PRAISE FOR *GET HIRED!*

Get Hired! is pure job search wisdom straight from the mouth of someone who has reached the goals you're working so hard to achieve. While other books have insights, this book gives you the straight-up truth about networking from one who has actually *done* it. Stop looking for better information—you'll find it right here! Jason has delivered another winner.
—**David Perry, Author of** *Guerrilla Marketing for Job Hunters 3.0*

I would definitely recommend this book to, well, literally AN-YONE. It is not a lightweight, rah-rah book; instead, it's weighty with wisdom, full of practical, sweat equity (mental AND physical) tips that you can start doing today. Perhaps you want to pull yourself out of the depths of a "dreary job search journey," or maybe you're currently employed but want to build strategic muscle that advances your future goals; either way, this book will provide the compass to propel you forward on your next-phase journey. Invest in this book—in these "career vitamins"—today!
—**Jacqui Barrett-Poindexter, Certified Master Resume Writer; CEO, CareerTrend.net**

Jason Alba's new book is a game-changer for anyone on the job hunt. With a clear, practical approach, Jason provides in-valuable guidance for navigating the competitive job market. His expertise shines through every page, making it a must-read for savvy professionals seeking to boost their careers. Jason's advice isn't just theory; it's a roadmap to success, ensuring you'll secure a better job more quickly.
—**Sarah Johnston, Job Search Strategist; Founder of The Briefcase Coach**

Clear, compelling, and compassionate, *Get Hired!* is an enormously helpful guide filled with "fundamental truths, not fads"—exactly what every job seeker needs to move from stuck to successful.
—Louise Kursmark, Master Resume Writer; Executive Career Consultant

Jason has demonstrated insight into what works today for successful job searching and a deep dedication to helping job seekers succeed in today's continuously evolving job search process. From Jason's amazing first book, *I'm on LinkedIn – Now What?* (one of the very first LinkedIn books!) to his sites that help job seekers successfully navigate the process (JibberJobber.com and JobSearchProgram.com), Jason has focused on helping job seekers to succeed. This amazing book continues that mission.
—Susan Joyce, President, NETability, Inc.; Publisher of Job-Hunt.org (1998–2021)

Today's job search can be daunting and job seekers typically don't know how it really works. Jason expertly walks you through each critical aspect, from personal branding, resume, LinkedIn profile, and other personal marketing content writing to networking, interviewing, and long term career management . . . with plenty of his own and others' job search highs and lows added in. His advice is actionable and easy to digest. By the final chapter, you'll be fully armed to land a job you deserve and find career fulfillment.
—Meg Guiseppi, Personal Branding and Executive Job Search Strategist; Founder of Executive Career Brand

In *Get Hired!*, Jason takes job seekers by the hand and walks them through the job search process step-by-step. Reading this should be the first step when starting a job search. *Get*

Hired! lays the foundation for an effective job search and for activities that will yield a high ROI. Every job seeker needs a copy!
—Jessica Hernandez, President, Great Resumes Fast

Jason's latest book has a wealth of great tips and useful information for job seekers. His perspective is inclusive, engaging, and fresh. I highly recommend you pick up a copy of *Get Hired!* as it will literally help you to get hired.
—Liz Handlin, CEO, Ultimate Resumes, LLC

Get Hired!

Jason Alba

Get Hired!

The Principle-Based Job Search Guide

PROFESSIONAL PATH PUBLISHING

ISBN 978-0-9853293-0-3 (paperback)

ISBN 978-0-9853293-2-7 (eBook)

ISBN 978-0-9853293-1-0 (audiobook)

Library of Congress Control Number: 2023921127

First edition 2024.

www.JibberJobber.com

To my wife and kids who have supported me since that life-changing layoff many years ago. And to every job seeker out there who has felt despair and loneliness.

CONTENTS

Get
Hired!

INTRODUCTION

This book has been years in the making. It all started when I was laid off from my job in 2006 and embarked on an epic job search. The intense effort I invested in trying to find a job made me intimately familiar with the unique challenges a job seeker faces, and during the process, I learned a lot. With the exception of my 10-month stint during 2018, I never actually found a job for myself. Rather than continuing my search for a corporate job, my job search inspired me to go in a different direction. I got to the point where I realized I needed to do my own thing, and immersed myself into the world of recruiters, career coaches, job search coaches, resume writers, and most importantly, job seekers. (Because I never actually landed a job, I now call my job search of 2006 my "Big Fat Failed Job Search.")

I used the experience I gained from fully throwing myself into my job search to start JibberJobber.com, a career management website that helps job seekers track and organize information about contacts they network with—who they talk with at which target company, what they talk about, and when they need to follow up. I've since written thousands of blog posts for job seekers. I wrote a few books, including, *I'm on LinkedIn—Now What?* which led to many professional speaking and consulting opportunities around the world. And I launched JobSearchProgram.com, which is a daily program where I give job seekers three important tasks to do each day to get them closer to their next job. I've also written guest posts for other bloggers, been paid to write about career ideas for industry experts, and been asked to contribute to articles for organizations such as Yahoo, AOL, and various news outlets.

My career path has taken a completely different trajectory than I expected. It's opened up so many opportunities and experiences I never could have imagined. I hope the things I've learned on my journey will be immensely helpful to you in landing your dream job, but also in helping you change how you think about your career, about life, about your value and purpose.

I've been thoughtful about career-related issues since I was a young boy, and since 2006, I've deeply immersed myself in the career space. This book is a collection of some of the most important ideas I've picked up, pondered, and put to the test over many years.

If you've picked this book up, chances are, you're going through a tough time right now. You may even be facing a serious life crisis. I've been there, and I'm here to help you through it.

Whether you find yourself searching for a job because you've been laid off or fired; or you're currently employed but want a job at a new company that values you more, pays what you think you are worth, or has values that match your own; or you want to change to a new career altogether . . . this book is for you. I will share with you eight time-tested principles—fundamental truths, not fads—to help you have an easier, more peaceful, and more effective job search. In addition to helping you figure out the next step in your career, these principles will guide you on how to manage your career throughout your working life.

Without further ado, let's jump in!

YOU NEED TO NETWORK WITH HUMANS

When I started my Big Fat Failed Job Search, which was a turning point in my career and the catalyst that led me to the path I'm on now, I treated "networking" as a four-letter word. It was unpleasant and something to be avoided. Perhaps worse, I thought I was too good to network. That is, I thought my resume, experience, background, tenacity, etc. would make up for any networking I wasn't doing.

I had no idea how networking would help my job search. I had no idea how it would change me.

Let me tell you about how I ended up at the first significant networking experience of my Big Fat Failed Job Search. It was a bumpy road filled with equal amounts of ego and self-doubt.

One day, walking down the hallway at church, I noticed a flier on a bulletin board advertising a job search networking club. The group had been around for years, but I never cared about or had reason to pay attention to it. I hadn't for a moment imagined I would ever need to attend something like that. Accomplished and successful people like me didn't need meetings like those (eye roll).

I made a mental note of where the meeting was held and resolved to go the very next Tuesday morning. After all, other than checking the job boards, I had nothing going on. By this point in my job search, getting up early, showering, getting dressed, and other forms of self-care were optional for me, especially before 1:00 pm. But Tuesday morning came along and I awoke early, showered, did my hair, dressed in nice clothes . . . the whole nine yards.

I drove to the area where I thought the networking meeting was being held, and guess what? It wasn't there! I had remembered the address wrong. So I drove around the neighborhood for a bit, putting in enough effort to at least feel good about trying, and then went home to stare at the job boards again.

The next week at church, I checked the flier and discovered I had gone to the wrong location. I wrote down the correct address, but when the day of the networking club arrived, I chickened out. I just couldn't bring myself to go to a meeting full of unemployed people. Why were they unemployed? What was wrong with them? Were they broken? Were they losers? Who really needed to go to a job search network meeting, anyway?

Not me.

It took a few weeks, but I finally got my act together and walked through the doors. The club met in a church, as most job clubs in the U.S. do. I went down the dark hallway to the room that had a light on and from which I could hear pleasant chatting. That was a long, hard walk. I didn't want to be there, but I was so close—I wasn't going to turn around and walk back to my car!

It had taken me a long time to get there, but I finally started my journey towards real networking.

I said this was my first significant networking experience. I finally allowed myself to seek out a networking opportunity because I realized that networking was an important strategy in my job search. Everyone knows, and studies confirm, that networking can significantly increase a person's chances of finding a job.[1]

But it's clear that networking isn't as important in certain sectors of the job market. I doubt 85% of fast food jobs are found through networking. Ever tried to get a job with the federal government? You generally don't network your way into those jobs.

Roles and levels are an important consideration. In my experience, the more advanced or specialized the job you are seeking is, the more important your networking efforts are. There are a lot of executive-level roles posted on job boards, but there's a big question about the validity of these posts. Career coaches, recruiters, hiring managers, and executives

I've talked to seem to agree that, often, these postings are only there to fulfill a posting requirement, a legality, while the hiring manager already knows (through their network) who they want to hire. In other words, they have already identified their first pick and maybe even made a verbal offer, but they need to post the opening just to comply with policy or law. How many job seekers are applying to postings that are already essentially closed?

THE HIDDEN JOB MARKET

Have you heard of the hidden job market? I'll let you in on the little secret I've discovered—the hidden job market isn't in any certain place. Here's how it works: A boss walks into a room with her team and says, "We just got approval to hire two more people. Do any of you know anyone who would be a great fit?"

This is a job on the so-called hidden job market. You can't Google it and you won't see it posted on job boards. No one knows about it except for a small group at the organization. Before they ever get around to posting the job, this group thinks about people they know who might be qualified and who they want to work with.

This scenario plays out in many organizations every day. The question is, how do you get in on the hidden job market? Well, if someone in that room knows about you, what you do, and what your technical strengths and proficiencies are, and they think you are a cool person and would become work friends with the team, they might bring up your name.

If they know about you!

It all comes down to networking and personal branding (which we'll get into in the next chapter).

Through networking, you get your name out there. If this is intimidating to you, don't worry. This chapter, and this book, are not just for extroverts who get excited about social interaction. I want you to know that even for an introvert, networking can be enjoyable, rewarding, and effective. I'll address this in more detail, but first, I want to share another significant takeaway I received from regularly attending that network meeting. I learned I was not alone in my dreary job search journey.

YOU'RE NOT ALONE

By the time I went to that network meeting, I had spent weeks, by myself, spinning my wheels. I had plenty of time to question how I got myself into that mess. I wondered what I could have done differently, and if I was really even qualified to have landed my previous job in the first place. During a career transition is a good time for self-reflection, but I found myself feeling defeated and focusing on all of my weaknesses, real and perceived.

If you've been in the rut of an ineffective job search long

enough, you understand what I was going through. You can be brutal to yourself. It doesn't help one bit that the constant rejection and non-response job seekers face seem to amplify negative self-talk. Salespeople may be used to rejection, but for the rest of us, receiving constant rejection during our job search may be one of the lowest points in our career, if not our life.

So imagine me, a few weeks into what was becoming a debilitating depression, thinking I was unqualified and maybe even an imposter in the professional world I'd lived in for years, sitting in a networking meeting with a bunch of other unemployed people. The moderator goes around the room inviting people to give their 30-second elevator pitch and, while I listen, I realize I'm sitting next to people with credentials and experiences similar to mine. Actually, there are people in the room who are way more qualified than I am.

It was that first meeting, and the next few, where I learned I wasn't there because I was unqualified or an imposter. I was there because, well, somehow I got there. But I certainly wasn't as bad as I'd been telling myself I was. I wasn't broken and neither was my career.

Going to that first network meeting saved me from giving up on the career I'd been working towards.

NETWORKING—A RELATIONSHIPS GAME

Let me tell you about the second experience that convinced me that networking was worthwhile. It was quite different from the first, but had an equal impact on changing networking from a four-letter word to something I realized was critical in my job search. This experience was reading the book, *Never Eat Alone,* by Keith Ferrazzi.[2] There are many books I recommend, but this is one of two that I always recommend when I speak to job seekers.

Never Eat Alone was the first book I read fast and slow at the same time. I read it quickly because I couldn't wait to get to the next chapter, the next idea, the next example. But I found myself reading it slowly, and rereading multiple parts, to make sure I fully understood what Keith was saying and internalize what I needed to learn about networking.

I was the perfect target audience. I was HUNGRY to change my circumstances. I learned a lot from this book and highly recommend you read it, and do so with a highlighter and pen in hand. While reading, I recommend you make a list of things you'll do to improve your networking.

Previously, I thought I had to go to conferences where there were lots of people and collect lots of business cards. That, I was led to believe, was the essence of networking. Lots of phone numbers and emails to follow up on. *Never Eat Alone* taught me, or rather gave me permission, to go to a lunch meeting with only one other person. I learned that lunch with one person, and the deep conversation we could have, could be way more impactful than a dozen superficial networking chats accompanied by the business cards I collected but never did anything with.

I went into my Big Fat Failed Job Search thinking networking was a numbers game. This book helped me understand networking is actually a relationships game. And relationships are not a one-time thing. Relationships are continual conversations with multiple touchpoints. It is following up with a purpose, even if that's just to check in and say "hi." When your networking goes beyond superficial to real relationships that span months, years, even decades, you are doing it right.

ADDING THE RIGHT PEOPLE TO YOUR NETWORK

As you network, consider these three characteristics when deciding if a networking contact is relevant to you:

1. Industry
2. Profession
3. Geography

This is a simple concept . . . if you meet someone or find someone online or in person who is in your industry or the industry you want to network into, in your profession (think job title) or adjacent to it, or is from any of the locations you are interested in, then they are relevant to you. These are the people you want to develop professional relationships with. Don't wait for them to reach out to you. If they are relevant to you, reach out to them and start a professional relationship.

NETWORKING TIPS

Here are three networking tips that will help you in your job search:

1. Become a Giver

I have networked long enough to have come across too many people who network for one reason: to take. They want to receive. They ask, they request, they take, and then they leave, seemingly without any consideration for the other person.

I've found job seekers to be a different kind of networker. I used to assume they were broken, losers, and there was a reason they didn't have a job. What I have found in the networking meetings I've been to is that many job seekers are in a special place in which they focus on giving. Sure, there are takers who don't give, but those are usually the newer job seekers. Once job seekers settle into a groove, and learn some networking etiquette, they start to give more than they take.

In one particularly memorable network meeting I spoke at, in Minnesota, each person shared their 30-second elevator pitch, including which companies they hoped to connect with. I was amazed as almost every single person received network referrals as soon as they finished sharing. For example, someone would say, "I'm looking for introductions into X, Y, and Z companies," and someone would walk across the room and say, "I had lunch with a product manager at Y company. Here's my card; I'll send an email introduction when I get home today."

Job seekers form a kind of camaraderie and become givers and sharers of information, contacts, even endorsements. The sooner you start to give to others, whether they are job seekers or not, the sooner you build what Keith Ferrazzi calls "relationship capital."[3] He says it's like a bank account where the more you deposit, the more you have to draw from later.

What I found is that the more I gave, the happier I was. I had more of a purpose in the meetings where I helped other people. I felt good about myself. During a time when you feel like you have very little to give or contribute, it's great to realize you can actually give something that can change someone's life and help pull them out of a dark place.

2. Follow Up

Keith Ferrazzi said something along the lines of, "If you want to be more successful than 95% of your competition, all you have to do is follow up."[4] It's that simple, and sad that so few job seekers do it. If you follow up, you will stand out.

Following up after you meet a networking contact is easy to do. You can follow up with an email or text, whichever you deem appropriate. If you want to go old school, send a note or card in the mail. Better to spend a few minutes on something that *might* not help you than being a candidate who didn't follow up.

Follow-up shows interest. It allows you to remind people who you are, perhaps highlighting strengths that are important to the job you are interested in. However simple your follow-up is, it can still have an impact on whoever you're following up with. Anything you do to stand out will help you during this process.

3. Initiate Informational Interviews

I describe informational interviews as having the right conversations with the right people. They are not job interviews, rather, they are networking conversations with specific objectives and components. They are a very strategic form of networking with the goal of getting you closer to a job offer.

I don't believe there's a silver bullet in the job search because there are so many circumstances that impact any solution or system. Declaring my system to be a silver bullet would be naive. However, I believe informational interviews done right are as close to a silver bullet as we'll ever get.

You can have informational interviews with anyone, really. I heard a story about a guy who called his grandma many states away, just to practice informational interviews. It turned out, his grandma knew someone at a company he was interested in working for; his grandma made an introduction and he ended up getting a job!

Through the informational interview process, you want to get introductions to people who can be influential in getting you into your next job. You might want to set up an informational interview with someone at your target company in your target role. Or you might want to set up informational interviews with people who don't work in your field or at target companies, but who might know someone who does. If you do informational interviews well, even a conversation with someone who seems disconnected from your target companies can be beneficial.

I recommend doing these in person, but a video call can be just as good and much more convenient for both parties.

To set up one of these valuable conversations, simply ask if you can have 30 minutes on their calendar—since if you asked them if you could have an informational interview with them, they might have no idea what you're talking about. You might say, "I'm going through a change in my career right now and noticed that you've worked in product management at XYZ Company for the last three years. I'd love to ask some questions about your role and what you've learned about product management since you've been there. Can we schedule a 30-minute meeting sometime this week?"

When I go to job clubs, I ask job seekers two questions about this topic. First, I ask who in the audience has heard of, and uses, informational interviews as a part of their job search strategy. Maybe 10% raise their hand. I am always surprised the number is so low. I would think every career expert who has spoken to them previously would have talked about informational interviews as a powerful strategy.

Next, of those who say they do informational interviews, I ask how many people are actually getting value out of doing them. Maybe one or two people raise their hands, and I continue to be shocked. I have written many posts on the JibberJobber blog about this topic, [5] and I created a Pluralsight course that goes into more depth.[6] I'll share the most important parts of getting value out of informational interviews here.

If I, who have been in the job search space for a long time, were to start a job search today, I'd spend 95% of my time on an informational interview strategy. Seriously, I think it's that important and that effective.

What most job seekers do wrong with informational interviews is they treat them like formal interviews. They make a list of questions they feel they need to ask, and they get anxious if they don't ask all, or most, of their questions. Being overly concerned about not asking every question is one of two big problems with failed informational interviews.

The second problem that many job seekers have is that when they go into an informational interview, they often act like there's a great class disparity between themself and the other person. Don't get me wrong, I think being respectful is important, but too often, I see job seekers act as if everyone who has a job is part of the upper class and they are part of the lower class.

I get it! I remember thinking that, as a job seeker, I was a third-class citizen. I wasn't contributing to society the way I would have been if I was currently employed and had a job with luxuries like a salary, a job title, perks, business cards, etc.

During my Big Fat Failed Job Search, I called an HR professional I had worked with on some software projects and asked him for advice about my job search. He warned me, "Jason, HR can smell blood from a mile away!"

I immediately thought about predators, like sharks and wolves, that can smell blood from a distance. My friend told me this because I was kind of whiny on our phone call. I was complaining, I was justifying why I was laid off (which is a mistake too many job seekers make), and I was, well, hurt. Honestly, I did not like this comment when he made it. I was offended—I thought he was a safe place for me to be whiny, open, and honest. But I realized he was right, so I took his advice to heart.

Those of you who are seeking a new job because you were laid off or fired may feel broken. You may feel slighted. You may have been wronged. And I know the roller coaster of emotions you are on. But I don't want you to think you are less than anyone you want to talk to. Sure, they might have an amazing job at an amazing company. They might even have the job you want at your top target company!

Even though you are a job seeker, you are not a third-, or even second-class citizen. You are just as good and competent as they are. You need to internalize this idea because if you go into every email, call, meeting, follow-up, etc. thinking you are less than, they'll know. And some people will not be willing to help you if they think you are too hurt.

When you ask for and do an informational interview, you need to respect who you actually are. You need to go in with confidence. Think about the informational interview as more of a conversation between two colleagues, two peers, two professionals, rather than an interview where you are hurt and broken and they are whole.

The last idea I want to share is that when you go into an informational interview, I recommend you do so with four objectives. Notice, the list does not include "make sure you ask all of your questions." It's good to be prepared with questions, but don't let them guide your meeting. Rather, let these four objectives guide your meeting.

Objective 1: Gather information

This sounds like you need to jump right in to asking your prepared questions, right? But actually, you can gather a lot of information without asking any of your questions. Pay attention to every single word they say. They may say something that gives you hints about what's happening at their organization or on their team. They may share information about the industry, like upcoming industry events you should know about, or current challenges that you should address in job interviews. Pay attention to everything they say and listen for any useful or relevant information.

Objective 2: Brand yourself

We'll talk about personal branding in the next chapter, but you need to know that informational interviews are a branding exercise. This is your chance to let someone who can help you in your job search know who you are. I'm not saying to treat the informational interview as a big commercial about you, but the interviewer will definitely walk away with an impression of you. You want to help them understand what your field is, what your roles or specialties are, and perhaps what kind of job or employer you are looking for. Be strategic about positively shaping their perception of you and intentionally portraying the right personal brand to them.

Objective 3: Develop professional relationships

Most people think networking is meeting people at conferences or meetups, talking to them, and hopefully getting an email or phone number. Maybe, just maybe, you'll have a follow-up conversation to start a long-term professional relationship with one of your new contacts. Networking sometimes feels like throwing spaghetti on the wall and seeing what sticks. It feels haphazard and unstrategic. Contrast that with informational interviews, which I call "networking on steroids" because they're not the superficial, collect-business-cards type of networking. Rather, they're intentional and strategic. One of the main objectives of every informational interview is to start a professional relationship you can nurture for years to come. If nothing else goes as planned, at least you will have spent time with this person and you can follow up later to keep that relationship going.

Objective 4: Obtain introductions

Receiving introductions from the interviewer to other potential employers is one of the most important objectives of every informational interview. A referral is helpful, but a warm introduction is always better. At a networking meeting I attended, someone shared a powerful idea: "You'll find your job leads from your third and fourth degree contacts, not your first and second degree contacts." By the time I heard it, I had gone through my first and second degree contacts and, surprise, none of them had any job leads for me! Hearing this idea helped me realize I needed to ask for more introductions, in order to get down to that third, fourth, and even fifth level.

The key to receiving good introductions is to help the other person trust you. Having a good, honest conversation with the interviewer will help develop trust. Being engaged in the conversation, taking notes, and asking relevant questions will help develop trust. People will feel more comfortable making introductions if they know you will follow through on each introduction. If you follow through within a day, and then follow up with the person who gave the introduction, you build trust and are likely to get more introductions.

If the time you spend in any informational interview accomplishes any of these four objectives, consider the meeting successful!

Your meeting might not go the way you expected or planned, and that is okay! This is not a one-and-done conversation— it is the first of hopefully many conversations you will have over years as you nurture this professional relationship.

Networking is vital to any job search, and informational interviews are a powerful networking tool that will be an important stepping stone in landing a job you will love. To learn more about informational interviews, check out my Pluralsight course or JibberJobber blog.

NETWORKING IN CASUAL CONVERSATION

A few years ago, I was frustrated that people seemed to want to help me and others in our job searches, but they didn't know how to help. Even more frustrating was the fact that we didn't know how to help them help us. That made the question, "How is your job search going?" uncomfortable because, well, if it was still going, then it wasn't going as well as I would have liked, right?

I came up with a brilliant response to this frequently asked question:

> "It's going well. I'm looking for introductions to anyone who works at some of my target companies. Do you know anyone who works at Company A, B, or C?"

By giving this response, you are answering the question they asked *and* the question that perhaps they wanted to ask but didn't vocalize, i.e., "How can I help you in your job search?" Notice, the response ends with a direct question that can be answered with a "yes" or a "no." I think it's important to ask a yes or no question because it's simple for the person to answer—it doesn't require them to think very hard.

Contrast that with, "Can you introduce me to someone who works at Company A, B, or C?" Now they have to think about not only if they know anyone well enough they could introduce you to, but also about whether they are comfortable making introductions for you and how to go about making the introduction. This could be too much of a mental load, overwhelming them and interfering with you receiving the results you want. So keep it simple and start with the yes or no question, "Do you know anyone who works at. . . ."

If they say "yes," then it's easy to move to that next step where you ask for an introduction. As you do this, you'll help others help you. Practice this every time someone asks you how your job search is going. Practice it with your accountability partner (discussed later), with your network groups, even with family and friends. If someone asks you how your job search is going, they are opening themselves up to this helpful response.

In sales there's an acronym, ABC, that stands for Always Be Closing. With job seekers, I change it a little to ABN: Always Be Networking. Practicing this question with people who know a lot about your job search, like your accountability partner, is important because things can change very quickly in a job search. Perhaps you start out looking at a certain role or targeting certain companies. Your focus can change daily.

Your accountability partner, and others in your network, think they know what you are looking for. For example, if you say you are looking for a project manager job, they are only going to be on the lookout for project manager jobs until you tell them differently. This becomes a problem when you are looking for more than one job title or role. If you are looking for a customer support manager or an operations manager role, but people think you are looking only for a customer support manager role, they won't think of you when they hear about an operations manager role. How do you help them best help you? You can change your response each time someone asks you how your job search is going. When you share that you are open to different roles, they are more likely to be on the lookout for more opportunities for you.

Same thing with the companies you are interested in working at. If the people you network with think you are only interested in jobs at XYZ company, they are going to be on the lookout for jobs only at XYZ company until you tell them differently. The next time they ask, or when it's appropriate in conversation, let them know you are open to jobs at additional companies.

SUMMING IT UP

If you are in a job search, you need to network! Going to networking meetings can be scary. But networking meetings are a great place not only to make new contacts to help in your job search, but also to understand just how normal it is to be in a job search. And as you increase your network, you have a better chance of getting into the hidden job market.

Networking isn't just for extroverts, it is for just about every job seeker. One-on-one meetings or conversations can be as effective, if not more effective, than going to big network meetings. Network with people who are relevant to you—people in your industry, profession, and/or location. Focus on giving, or adding value, to people in your network, following up, and doing informational interviews. Finally, remember to be strategic in the way you answer common questions you get as a job seeker, especially the question, "How's your job search going?"

NOTES

[1] Lou Adler. "New Survey Reveals 85% of All Jobs are Filled Via Networking." LinkedIn. February 28, 2016. https://www.linkedin.com/pulse/new-survey-reveals-85-all-jobs-filled-via-networking-lou-adler.

[2] Keith Ferrazzi & Tahl Raz. *Never Eat Alone: And Other Secrets to Success, One Relationship at a Time.* New York: Penguin Group, 2005/2014.

[3] Keith Ferrazzi & Tahl Raz, *Never Eat Alone.*

[4] Keith Ferrazzi & Tahl Raz, *Never Eat Alone.*

[5] See https://blog.jibberjobber.com/?s=informational+interviews.

[6] See https://www.pluralsight.com/courses/informational-interviews.

PEOPLE NEED TO UNDERSTAND WHO YOU ARE

I need to throw out a disclaimer regarding the previous chapter: Networking is not the only way people land jobs. I remember after I started JibberJobber and was a strong advocate of the power of networking, I went to lunch with a guy I had just met. He had recently landed an awesome job at an awesome company. I was so excited that as soon as we sat down, I asked him to tell me the story of how he landed such a great role. I was sure I knew the answer!

And, I was totally wrong. Very nonchalantly, almost bored, he said, "Well, I applied on [a certain popular job board], got an interview, and then an offer. It was easy and had nothing to do with networking."

While networking is really important, there are other tactics and tools I will discuss throughout this book to use in your job search to help you find, and land, the right role for you. And your personal branding is a big part of it.

Personal branding is one of my favorite topics because of how important the right personal brand is in a job search.

I learned about the power of personal branding the hard way. When I started my job search, I had a personal brand, but it wasn't the right one for the job I wanted. I wanted to get a local job, but I had spent the previous 18 months working at a very small company in an industry that had no local clients, which meant anyone who knew who I was didn't live in our area. Meanwhile, my competition had gone to college, maybe even high school, in the area. Local hiring managers knew who they were.

I knew that to get a local job, I needed to do something to get my name out there. I was familiar with the basic tools everyone knows all too well, like resumes, a LinkedIn profile, cover letters, and other personal marketing assets, but when I learned about personal branding, and how it goes hand in hand with networking, my eyes were opened to a better way to find a great job.

Since then, I have spoken a lot about personal branding. I consider it one of three critical elements of career management (the other two are networking and creating multiple streams of income, to have what I call income security, as opposed to job security). On one particular occasion, I was speaking about personal branding to a group of MBA candidates at a prestigious university on the West Coast. One of the speakers before me spent her entire session speaking about personal branding. I was glad I saw her presentation so I could avoid sharing the same information she shared. What happened after her presentation, though, would become an important part of my own understanding of personal branding. I overheard a student walking out of the auditorium say to another, "I still have no idea what personal branding is." After a presentation that was more than an hour long, this MBA student, who I do not doubt is highly intelligent, given the university he was attending, didn't understand the basic concept of personal branding.

How was this possible? As I considered this, I realized that although I could easily speak about personal branding for an hour or two, I didn't really know how to succinctly summarize it either!

Until right then, when it came to me. Personal branding, I now say, is simply how others perceive you.

HOW OTHERS PERCEIVE YOU

This very short phrase, "how others perceive you," is more powerful than you might imagine. Too often, people think personal branding is how they describe themselves. What their tagline is, or their 30-second elevator pitch. They can spend hours on personal branding exercises to understand who they are and come up with some very clever branding statements. But no matter what you do, say, or intend, people might perceive you completely differently.

Perhaps you think your brand is that you are a great

salesperson, programmer, product manager, or strategist. But people might perceive you to be forward and grumpy. What you do professionally might not even matter because the prominent parts of your brand are those characteristics.

Have you worked with someone who was super nice or cool? Or someone who was a jerk, someone you wouldn't want to work with again? That's part of your perception of them, which means that, at least for you, that is part of their brand.

Sure, maybe the jerk is awesome at what they do, but if you don't want to work with them again, you won't recommend them when you hear about openings.

What this means for you is that you need to figure out how others perceive you, how you want them to perceive you, and how to help change their perceptions. If people perceive you in a way you don't want them to, figure out whether this is a communication issue or whether you need to change something about yourself. For example, if you are great at building high-performing teams but people think you are not a good leader, maybe you need to communicate or somehow demonstrate better that your teams are high performing in order to validate your leadership skills.

On the other hand, if you are indeed not a great leader, work on becoming a better leader. Read books on empathy, results-oriented leadership, and anything else you can get your hands on to improve your leadership skills. Perhaps work on your one-on-ones with your team and make them more valuable for each person. If you're currently not employed, you can practice being a better leader in your family or in community groups. Get a mentor or coach, and do anything else you can to improve your leadership.

Evaluating negative perceptions or misunderstandings to determine whether you need to communicate better or grow in those areas can help you focus on the right things as you work to improve your personal brand.

To understand how others perceive you, simply ask them. One great way to do this is by using what is sometimes called a 360 survey. You can do it one-on-one, either in person or using technology (like email or Google forms).

When you ask a person how they perceive you, they might worry that how they perceive you is not how you want to be perceived, and they may worry about hurting your feelings. So you need to make it clear to them that you want them to be completely honest with you. Honest responses are the only responses that will help you on your personal branding journey.

If you are self-aware, you already have a good idea how others perceive you. But it never hurts to ask others. Make sure you get input from a variety of people in your network. Borrowing from the 360 survey model, you want to get input from more than just friends and more than just customers. For example, ask your colleagues and people you have reported to. People you had a different working relationship with will have different perspectives of you and your work. The types of people I recommend you ask include peers/colleagues, superiors (supervisors, bosses, and other leaders in organizations you've worked at), customers, and people you've managed. Of course, you can also include neighbors, family members, people you volunteer with, etc.

The idea is to get as much of a whole picture as you can. Some input will be reassuring or validating, while other input may be hard to hear because it is either new, negative, or validates some of your insecurities. That's okay. This process, however difficult, will help you understand yourself better and can help you grow in areas where you need to.

It's important that you don't take this feedback personally, in a destructive way. Hearing negative or hard things about yourself can be demoralizing, but when people open up, are honest, and give you hard-to-hear feedback, they really are giving you a gift. You need to recognize they are actually risking their relationship with you, even their standing with you, when they share this information. Be appreciative, even if what they say helps you realize you have some work to do to be a better person or help others have a better perception of you.

Usually, most of the feedback you'll get will be positive, especially if the people you ask know you are in the middle of a job search. Listen to every word they tell you and look for patterns or themes. If people continually remark that you are really nice, funny, dependable, or whatever, make note of that. That is how others perceive you, and that is a part of your brand!

Take the good parts of this feedback and start to craft a brand profile. Include your hard skills (for example, technical proficiencies) as well as your soft skills (for example, how you work with others). These are things you can easily build into your brand messaging. For example, you can include the feedback when you talk about yourself: "People I work with say I'm really easy to get along with and I'm one of the most dependable colleagues they've worked with."

LET OTHERS TALK ABOUT YOU

Ah, did you catch that? This is perhaps one of the coolest things I realized as I embarked on my own personal branding journey. Let me back up a little.

Many people have a hard time talking about themselves. We have been taught, from a very young age, that it is impolite to brag about ourselves. If you are outside of the U.S., bragging about yourself is probably even more offensive.[1]

Brag! The Art of Tooting Your Own Horn Without Blowing It, is an excellent book on this critical aspect of personal branding.[2] Perhaps the most important takeaway I received from this book was permission. I felt like I needed permission to talk about myself in a positive way.

35

Guess what? As a job seeker you will have plenty of opportunities to talk about yourself. You'll be in a network meeting and someone will say, "Tell me about yourself." You'll be in a job interview and they'll ask you to introduce yourself. You'll be at lunch with a friend who introduces you to someone and they'll ask you to share a little about what you are doing or looking for. Sometimes you get to plan and prepare for these conversations, like if you are attending a network meeting, but at other times, the opportunities are spontaneous.

Often, people introduce themselves with self-deprecation, either because they feel insecure or want to be humble, or in an attempt to diffuse stress with humor. I challenge you, as a job seeker, to move away from this tactic and move towards self-confidence. Figure out positive things to say about yourself and avoid downplaying your strengths or insulting yourself.

Okay, so let's say you know what you want to say about yourself. Let's say that, even though you've read *Brag!* you are still uncomfortable speaking positively about yourself. That's okay. Consider how these two statements feel coming out of your mouth and how they likely come across to others:

> "I am a great team-player—I work well with others."
>
> vs.
>
> "People say I am a great team player and work well with others."

The first one feels, and sounds, like someone bragging about themselves in a weird way. I mean, they are just stating what they perceive to be as facts, but I'd question that. As an interviewer I'd want to dig into that a bit and understand what they are basing that statement off of. The second statement, though, comes with some authority. Other people are saying it. It's like there are other witnesses who would go to bat for you and say that yes, indeed, you are a great team player.

You haven't provided citations or phone numbers, but just by saying people say that about you, this statement feels more credible. And, it's easier to say. There are other ways to say this, like:

- "People I work with say . . ."
- "People I've reported to have said . . ."
- "My bosses say . . ."

I mentioned the 360 survey as a way to collect this type of information. Another way to get this information is in a LinkedIn Recommendation. Because of the way Recommendations are set up, you can't create fake testimonials. However, you can do the heavy lifting for your contacts. I recommend you (a) ask for a Recommendation on LinkedIn, and (b) give your contact an idea of what you want them to include. You could do this by giving them a bulleted list of things you want them to talk about, or you could provide them with an example Recommendation and tell them they can use it or edit it if they would like to. People are busy. Writing something like this for you takes time and creative effort. By providing them with a list of ideas or an example Recommendation, you help make their life easier. And you also lessen the risk that they will omit the things you would like them to say.

Does that approach sound disingenuous? Consider this: It is not uncommon to ask for a letter of recommendation from your boss and have your boss say, "Write one up and I'll make my edits." Seriously. Once a boss, trying to help me out, wrote me a letter of recommendation which was more of an apologetic explanation of why he laid me off than it was a recommendation of me or my capabilities. When I asked him for a rewrite (which was awkward), he asked me to write it and he'd simply sign it. That way, it would say what I wanted it to say. As I've talked about this with JibberJobber users and people in my job club audiences, I've come to realize this kind of thing is more common than I previously thought.

There's power in having the right messaging and sharing the positive things other people are saying about you.

PERSONAL MARKETING ASSETS

There are many personal marketing assets you can use to help create and share your personal brand. I will discuss some of the more common ones below.

Resumes

When most people start a job search, the first thing they figure they need to do is put together a resume. A resume is a funny beast. When I began my job search, I didn't understand what a resume was really used for, or how it could be optimized, and so I did what most people do: I downloaded a resume template and tried to flesh it out. The resulting resume was . . . ordinary. And from what I've seen, ordinary is not good. Ordinary is probably just enough, but no professional marketer shoots for "just enough."

Even with the ever-popular LinkedIn profile, the resume still seems to be a main marketing asset for job seekers. I thought I couldn't really start my job search without one. I thought I couldn't network without one. You don't have to pause everything while you are trying to figure out all the details of your resume—what font to use, how much to indent, how to phrase your experiences, etc. You *can* start your job search without a resume. But you'll likely be asked for it sooner rather than later, and may find yourself stuck without one, so get your resume done. Get it out. Get it ready to use.

If you can find the money, I strongly encourage you to find a trained resume writer (there are a few associations for career professionals, and, more specifically, resume writers, that list their members and the members' credentials, such as the National Resume Writers' Association, Career Thought Leaders, Career Directors International, and the

Professional Association of Resume Writers and Career Coaches).

My Resume Mistake

The main purpose of your resume is to get you into an interview. If you are not getting interviews, take a look at your resume. Better yet, have a professional resume writer take a look at your resume. Often, we work on our own resumes so much we can't see them the way someone else does. A professional resume writer can look at it with fresh eyes and has the benefit of years of experience looking at hundreds or thousands of resumes. This allows them to zero in quickly on exactly what your resume needs to get noticed and secure the interview you want.

At the start of my Big Fat Failed Job Search, when I was clueless about how to find a job and feeling discouraged, I turned to my dad for support. He said, "Hey, I just paid a lot of money for a resume writer to write my resume. I'll send it to you and you can change it to work for yourself."

Great intentions. I saved money and he got double the value, right? Anyone in the career space who is reading this is thinking, "What an idiot. You should never do that!"

But being the unenlightened job seeker I was, I took my dad up on the offer and modified his expensive resume with my information. I changed this and that and that and this and slowly transformed the resume into a resume for me. And I began applying to jobs.

By that point, I'd decided I wanted to go a little deeper into the individual contributor path and get more experience there. I searched for business analyst and project manager jobs. I was surely qualified, given my experience and education, to do either of those. My three previous titles before I got laid off were IT Manager, CIO/VP of IT, and General Manager. But I was not applying for those jobs, or jobs at those levels. See the problem?

Imagine you are a recruiter, or someone involved in the screening process, and you see a resume for someone who had any of those three titles for the past few years applying to a job that seems like a significant step down. There could be a legitimate reason for applying to a lower-level job— perhaps the candidate is ready to take a break from management and go back to an individual contributor role. Maybe the candidate likes the work in those jobs more, doesn't want management responsibility, or, as in my case, is interested in beefing up their skills in the new role.

Whatever the reason, all the recruiter knows is that they have a hundred, or hundreds, of candidates to screen and there are a lot of people who have customized their resume so they appear to be a great fit for that specific opening.

I am sure I customized my cover letters, but even so, I might have appeared to be a washed-up executive, and they had plenty of other applicants who appeared to be a better fit than me. There was enough of a mismatch to cause the screener to click "No" on my application.

My mistake was that I didn't understand I needed to fit the resume to the job title and description I was applying to. I could have easily removed my leader titles and generically put "manager" or other descriptors that watered the titles down a little. Doubtless, I would have had better results if I had engaged a professional resume writer who would have been able to look at my situation and identify why I wasn't getting into interviews. Instead, I spent a lot of months spinning my wheels doing the wrong thing.

I don't know what your resume problems are, or will be. There are plenty of possibilities, from cliched grammar and spelling issues to creating a resume that is too short or too long. Maybe you are using a chronological format when you should be using a functional format, or vice versa. Maybe you are so focused on getting the facts right that you don't realize you are not appropriately communicating your accomplishments.

These problems are all typical. If you have more time than money, I recommend you spend some time learning all you can about how to craft a great resume. Read resume books and pore over articles and other resources that you can find from resume association websites or a simple internet search to learn what you need to do to make sure your resume gets you into interviews.

One final thought about your resume: Your resume is not your obituary. An obituary is backwards facing. It tells about what a person did, their past accomplishments, etc. It is a reflection. A resume needs to be forward facing, which means it should be written for the role you are applying to. If your resume is written like an obituary, you may end up with more offers to do work you've already done, rather than the work you want to do.

Remember, your resume is a marketing tool with the purpose of getting you an interview for a job. You want to customize your resume for the job you want to land instead of for the jobs you've already had. Yes, include relevant information from your history, but if something isn't relevant, either remove it or give it less space.

As someone who has been involved in the hiring process many times, I can tell you that if I'm looking for A, B, and C on a resume, that's exactly what I need to see on your resume in order for you to land an interview. Don't make me do the mental gymnastics of trying to figure out how your D, E, and F logically follow A, B, and C, especially when other resumes scream A, B, and C.

You may dislike resumes. Remember, they are simply a tool. They are one aspect of a very complex process. Craft a great resume, customize it for each job, and then move on to other parts of your job search.

Other Personal Marketing Assets

Your resume is just one of your personal marketing assets; other assets might include your tagline, business cards, LinkedIn profile, 30-second elevator pitch, personal website, and maybe a blog or book. I will discuss each of these in greater detail below. Note—it's a great idea to provide links in your resume to some of your other marketing assets, which helps someone vetting you learn much more about you than what you're able to share with them in the limited space on your resume.

Your Tagline

Your tagline serves as your primary claim. Every other bit of personal branding you do should tie back to, and reinforce, your tagline.

Personal taglines are so versatile—they can be used in a networking conversation, in a job search interview, during an informational interview, on your resume, in your email signature, on your blog, in a byline for an article you write . . . just about anywhere! A tagline should be a very short phrase and does not need to be a complete sentence. For example, "award-winning account manager" or "programmer who also talks to humans" are two taglines that communicate a lot in a short phrase.

Avoid using jargon or cliches in your taglines. Too often I see people try to create something catchy, but the jargon or cliche they use is confusing. For example, "I'm here to excel" doesn't tell me anything about your role, results, or what you can do for me. "I'm a go-getter!" does nothing to instill confidence that you achieve results, go above and beyond, or anything else I'd expect from a go-getter.

A powerful tagline should be easy to understand, even by people who are not familiar with your role. This will help them recognize if you might be a match for any roles they are hiring for and will help them talk about you to others more effectively.

Business Cards

Some people think using business cards is outdated. But despite the proliferation of smartphones, which allow people to easily share their contact information when networking, business cards are still widely used. If you do any face-to-face networking, I strongly encourage you to get business cards so that you have something tangible to leave behind with new contacts. Your business card should be simple and, as with taglines, free from jargon and cliches. Include only the most important information, such as your contact information and your tagline.

If your business card is a personal business card used solely in your job search, you can include something like "Target roles I'm interested in." A job search business card is a tool to help others know how they can best help you, and they can help you better when they understand what kind of role you are looking for.

Vistaprint.com is a great, inexpensive business card design builder and printer.

Your LinkedIn Profile

The LinkedIn profile has almost become the de facto

resume. It hasn't completely replaced the resume, though, and I don't think it ever will, but it's become so pervasive in networking and the job search that not having one seems suspicious to employers.

Don't worry about making your LinkedIn profile perfect. Just spend a few minutes on it each day until you feel like it is good enough.

While the resume has rather rigid rules (such as length, what to include, verb tenses, formatting, etc.), the LinkedIn profile is a lot more flexible. Here are my top tips to enhance your profile:

- Provide a high quality, professional photograph of yourself. I recommend something with good color contrast, and something that looks good in a very small area, for example, when someone is looking at a list of profile pictures on their phone.
- Include your tagline in the "headline" section, which shows up directly under your avatar. You can include more than your tagline, if it helps clarify your brand, breadth, or depth (breadth and depth are discussed later in this chapter), but make sure your primary claim is front-and-center.
- Use as many of the 2,000 characters in the description, job details (experience), and education sections as you can. You can include mini-stories here as well as keywords that you think recruiters,

business owners, and hiring managers will search for (such as "senior product manager" or "customer service manager").

Since you can't customize your LinkedIn profile for different roles like you can with resumes, you need to make your profile more general. You can link to relevant resources, such as specific articles, your website, even your resume(s). In this way your LinkedIn profile becomes a landing page with great information that helps your audience learn more about you.

Your 30-Second Elevator Pitch

The elevator pitch is a common statement job seekers are encouraged to create and memorize to use in networking and interviews. "Hi, my name is Jason Alba. I'm a product manager with 16 years of experience in the software industry. I've worked for. . . ."

As suggested by its name, this statement is typically around 30 seconds long. It's called an "elevator pitch" because it's the perfect length to share when you have a short period of time to deliver it, like during an elevator ride. I've been to network meetings for job clubs where someone has a stopwatch and times you. If you go past 30 seconds they will stop you! I don't think you need to be that strict, although being concise should definitely be a goal.

One of the most important things to consider when creating your elevator pitch, as with your resume, is making it a forward-facing marketing tool. Instead of focusing on past roles, if they're not aligned with the role you are looking for, focus on the most important characteristics you want to bring out to help you get the role you want.

For example, "I'm Jason Alba and I've been in the tech industry for over 20 years. While I've spent most of my time as a developer and product manager, I have extensive experience supervising technical teams and creating strategies for high-growth tech companies. I am passionate about building and supporting efficient technical teams and have essentially served as CIO of my last two organizations. I am looking for a CIO position in a growing tech company that needs strong leadership and vision."

The biggest hang-up I have with elevator pitches is that they can sound robotic and impersonal. Sometimes people focus on saying every word exactly right and sound strained when they repeat it. Practice your elevator pitch enough that it sounds natural and people believe you are excited about what you are saying. And be prepared to improvise if the situation calls for it.

Your Website and/or Blog

It's easy, and inexpensive, to get a personal website. First, buy a domain at godaddy.com, hopefully one that includes your name or job title. Prior to creating a personalized website, you can redirect your domain to your LinkedIn profile. There are a number of legitimate web services that allow you to create and host your own website, free of charge or very inexpensively. These include wordpress.com, squarespace.com, and wix.com. Your website can be as simple as you want it to be, but if you are in the graphic arts space, realize that your website will be your portfolio, too.

The most important thing is to not get overwhelmed with the amazing personal branding sites (or portfolios) out there. You can have a very effective personal website that communicates your brand well, and helps people understand your professional passions, expertise, experience, and brand messaging, without the amazing graphics that some artists are able to create.

Also, I am an advocate of using a blog—a blog is one of the best personal branding tools. You can blog on your personal website (all the websites I listed above have blogging functionality built into them). Your blog is essentially a place where you write and store articles for others to see. Does it matter if barely anyone reads your blog? Maybe only six people (including some close friends or relatives) will actually read it, but what if one of those six people is the hiring manager for the job you just applied for? If you have great content on your blog, you might just land an interview instead of being passed over.

Blogging can be a long-term commitment, but it can also be just a dozen blog posts that communicate what you want to communicate about your brand. A prospective employer won't read hundreds of your blog posts, but if they see a dozen blog posts with thoughtful titles and relevant topics, that might be enough to impress them and make them want to learn more about you.

Other Articles

In addition to any blog posts you might write for your own website, on other sites, you can publish one-off articles that help share your personal brand and professional expertise. There are plenty of websites that will let you write articles for free like LinkedIn, Medium.com, and DEV.to for developers.

You could also pitch articles to industry newsletters. Some industry associations who have a newsletter or magazine regularly look for experts to share insights, perspectives, experiences, and predictions. Other times, they might want a fee for publishing an article, but having an article published in a widely read industry publication might be worth it.

Every article you write should reinforce your brand, supporting who you are and what you can do for an employer.

For example, if you are a marketing professional, you could write an article about the five most important skills a marketing professional needs to excel in their career. Or an article with your three predictions of how economic changes will impact marketers in your industry in the coming year. Or, four lessons from this past year that every marketer needs to pay attention to.

The idea is to create content that shows you have expertise in and passion about areas that are relevant to the role you are looking for. Once you have written the articles, share them. In a job search interview, you could say, "I wrote an article on this very topic. I'll send you a link later today."

Writing a Book

I'm a loud advocate of writing a book to enhance your personal brand. Professional speakers I've talked to say their book is their "very expensive business card" because a business card could cost a few cents while a book could cost a few dollars, per book, to get printed. The great thing about publishing a book is that as it shares important information with the world, it also makes it clear that you are an expert in your field. When people discover that you have written a book relevant to your industry, it will establish you as an authority and make you more desirable as an employee.

If the idea of writing a book feels intimidating, let me simplify it. Your book could be nothing more than a 20-page eBook. Does writing 20 pages seem like too much work? Double space the text, add pictures (you can find royalty-free images from pexels.com or unsplash.com), and maybe even increase the font size. Really, your book does not need to be as long as many of the papers students write in ordinary university classes.

What should your book be about? I recommend writing a book that would be interesting to people in the role you are hoping to be hired for. For example, if you are looking for a senior product manager job, the title might be "5 Things Every Senior Product Manager Needs to Know." Imagine how impactful it can be in a job interview if you respond to a question with, "I've actually written a book that talks about this topic. I'll send you a copy." You will surely stand out as someone who is passionate about the topic and, as an author, have some credibility as an expert in product management.

Once you have written and edited your book, save it as a PDF, then share it. It's that simple. You can upload it to your website, or you can even self-publish it on Amazon—if you're up for learning something new, it isn't that difficult.

After you put your book out there for the world, be sure to add your book to your resume and LinkedIn profile and indicate that you are an author.

YOUR BREADTH AND DEPTH

One of the reasons you need more personal marketing assets than just a resume is because while your resume does a great job for its very specific purpose, it does a very poor job of communicating, or representing, your breadth and depth.

Your "breadth" means the wide variety of your strengths, abilities, skills, characteristics, etc. For example, let's say you are a senior manager. Your breadth will likely include the ability to read and understand P&Ls, build powerful teams, lead teams to excellence, negotiate with and persuade executives, work with customers, etc.

You should be able to list the elements of your breadth for whatever role you are working towards. Understanding the breadth of skills required and the breadth of what you have to offer can help you understand how much of a match, or mismatch, a particular role is for you.

If you put these skills and characteristics across the top of a sheet of paper or spreadsheet, you can identify your "depth" by diving into each of them and quantifying your expertise, experience, and exposure. For example, if one of your breadth skills is working with customers, your depth might include the number of years you have directly worked with customers, your ability to save customer relationships, your customer service scores or feedback, and anything else that shows your experience with customers.

I once received a resume from a university student claiming proficiency in about 15 programming languages. I remember looking at that and thinking, "There is no way he is proficient in 15 programming languages." Actually, what I really thought was, "Just because you read an article about Java doesn't mean you can put Java on your resume!" Maybe this kid really was a genius, but what I read on his resume turned me off to him. I made my decision about him before he came in.

If that sounds petty to you, perhaps it is. But I promise you, this kind of assessment is happening with your own marketing assets. People will hear you say something, or read something you wrote in an email, cover letter, resume, or online application, and make a judgment. That's what we do, we judge. This is called making a judgment call and it happens all day, every day, everywhere.

You have to figure out how to create the right marketing assets for yourself in order to avoid being negatively judged or stereotyped. Understanding and appropriately communicating your breadth and depth can help you get past those initial screenings and get to a place where you can make a stronger argument for yourself as the right hire.

SUMMING IT UP

When you understand who you are, how you want to be perceived, and how others currently perceive you, you have the information you need to work on your personal brand. Creating and sharing various types of personal marketing assets will help people understand who you are, how they can help you, or why you are a fit for their job opportunity. You can have more fun in your job search because your message is aligned with what you are looking for, helping you focus on the roles that will be the best fit for you.

I hope this chapter has inspired you to get serious about your personal branding strategy. Personal branding is a broad topic. There are lots of books, articles, podcasts, and other resources you can seek out to help you further improve your personal branding. I even offer a course on personal branding at Pluralsight.[3] Work on the personal marketing assets you are weak on. And make sure your messaging is clear and aligned with the direction you want to go.

NOTES

---

[1] Dorie Clark & Andy Molinsky. "Self-Promotion for Professionals from Countries Where Bragging Is Bad." *Harvard Business Review*, March 21, 2014. https://hbr.org/2014/03/self-promotion-for-professionals-from-countries-where-bragging-is-bad.

[2] Peggy Klaus. *Brag! The Art of Tooting Your Own Horn Without Blowing It.* New York: Warner Business Books, 2003.

[3] See https://www.pluralsight.com/courses/developing-killer-personal-brand.

YOU NEED TO BE ACCOUNTABLE

BEING ACCOUNTABLE TO YOURSELF

Below, I'll talk about the importance of enlisting an accountability partner, but at the end of the day, the most important person you need to be accountable to in your job search is yourself. You need to be honest with yourself about your efforts and what you are doing. But do so with self-compassion—avoid the tendency to be honest to the point of cruelty. We tend to beat ourselves up for not achieving our often unrealistic expectations without celebrating our accomplishments. Strive for a healthy perspective.

One way to be accountable to yourself is to create a spreadsheet or other system to track your progress. I love to use the conditional formatting function in Google Sheets or Excel to color code my progress. For example, let's say I set a goal to reach out to five new people every day. I could set up a spreadsheet that tracks how many people I talk to. When the number of people talked to in a day exceeds five, the cell, through conditional formatting, turns green.

Gamifying my spreadsheet in this way provides fun motivation.

Other tasks you may want to track include the number of informational interviews and job interviews you do, the number of new target companies you add to your list, follow-ups, etc.

Should you use a self-accountability system instead of being accountable to another human? I'd say do both. The system you use to track your progress can also be a great tool to share with your accountability partner so they can see the real, raw numbers. And the system can last through multiple accountability partners. Speaking of accountability partners. . . .

ENROLL AN ACCOUNTABILITY PARTNER

Can you be accountable to yourself *instead* of an accountability partner? Yes, for sure. But I find it is too easy to slip into bad habits, skip the hard things, and otherwise be much less effective in my tasks if I don't have someone I know I'm going to report to regularly. On the other hand, when I know someone is going to ask me, "Did you do that task?" I work on that task, even if it's in the few hours before we meet.

During my Big Fat Failed Job Search, it was easy for me to conceptually understand the importance of enrolling an accountability partner to help me in my job search, but it was difficult for me to implement. It was difficult to swallow my pride and admit I needed help. And figuring out the logistics was overwhelming and seemed like more trouble than it was worth.

I couldn't have been more wrong—I definitely would have benefited from having an accountability partner in my job search!

I've come to learn that just about every career coach recommends every job seeker have an accountability partner. Even so, I rarely see people who utilize an accountability partner. Having an accountability partner is one of the most important parts of a successful job search strategy.

WHAT DOES ACCOUNTABILITY LOOK LIKE?

Ideally, you will check in with your accountability partner daily, or at least weekly. If you check in less than weekly, you'll likely lose momentum in your job search. This reporting doesn't have to be in person. It could be through a phone call, video call, email, or text message.

Let me emphasize, though, that the more personal your interactions are, or the less you communicate with your accountability partner through faceless technology (like sending a text with a quick report), the more you'll nurture the relationship. There is value in having an accountability partner who you can trust with the more human aspects of your job search.

While your accountability partner can be a counselor or coach, they don't have to be. It's much easier to find someone who isn't formally trained. While they aren't necessarily there to provide therapy or definitive coaching, they will likely help in both of those areas. During what can feel like a very lonely job search, the relationship can be lifesaving.

Your accountability partner might also help you network. The more people there are who know about what roles you are interested in and what your target companies are, the more people there are who can help you.

CHOOSING AN ACCOUNTABILITY PARTNER

Who you choose to be your accountability partner makes a big difference. For starters, like a few of my career professional friends say:

> "YOUR ACCOUNTABILITY PARTNER CAN-NOT BE YOUR SIGNIFICANT OTHER!"

Your accountability partner cannot, or a very strong should not, be someone too close to you. A significant other, a spouse, even a parent or other close relative, can be too close to the emotional roller coaster and too emotionally involved in the outcome. And, you are going to need a good support system away from your job search to just be human—to laugh with you, to chill with you, to listen to your woes. Separate the roles of emotional support partner and accountability partner because you will need both, especially if your job search drags on longer than you expect.

There are two critically important characteristics you need in an accountability partner. First, they need to be the type of person who will hold you accountable. Sounds obvious, but sometimes you find someone you are comfortable with and discover they are not able to ask the hard questions you need to be asked. Second, they need to be up to date on current job search tactics. Imagine, for example, you ask your 70-year-old grandmother to be your accountability partner. I don't have anything against 70-year-old grandmas, but I'm guessing that she is not current on job search strategies and tools. Your accountability partner shouldn't encourage you to conduct your job search as you would have thirty years ago.

That's not to say that there aren't any 70-year-olds who would be great accountability partners. I know career professionals in their 70s who are up to date on the job search scene. Dick Bolles was 90 when he died, and my understanding is he worked on the latest edition of what has been perhaps the most famous job search book ever, *What Color Is Your Parachute?* right up to the end of his life.

Alternatively, you could find someone your age, or significantly younger, who is so disconnected from what makes a job search effective, especially a job search for someone at your level in your industry, that they would be a poor accountability partner.

You can find accountability partners in your family (as long as it is not a spouse, or anyone too emotionally invested in the outcome), among past colleagues, perhaps even among associates you volunteer with. Fellow job seekers can make great accountability partners because they are very interested in current job search strategies and tactics since they are in the thick of their own job search. They are also empathetic towards job seekers. They understand the importance of what you are doing and should be able to easily grow in their role as your accountability partner.

Network meetings for job seekers are a great place to find accountability partners. As you connect with people, be on the lookout for someone you are comfortable with and who seems like would make a great accountability partner.

TRAINING YOUR ACCOUNTABILITY PARTNER

When you ask someone to be your accountability partner, you'll probably find they are willing, but they don't know what they need to do in that role. It's your job to help them know what to do. It's also your job to do most of the heavy lifting in the relationship. You are responsible for choosing which tactics you use in your job search and creating whatever tracking system you decide to use, whereas your accountability partner is there simply to help you do what you know you need to do.

Their main job is to hold you accountable. When you bring on an accountability partner, explain your job search system to them, the daily tasks you need to do, and that you would like to regularly report to them so they can help keep you on track. Ideally, you, as the person with the most interest in changing your situation, will proactively report to them, but let them know that if you don't, you'd like them to be proactive in asking, "Did you do the five things you said you were going to do this week?"

In order for working with an accountability partner to be beneficial, you need to be completely honest, even when you don't complete the tasks you planned to do. There is no shame in falling short sometimes. I expect you will be so motivated to change your situation that you'll put the work in. The accountability factor in your job search is not meant to shame you, rather to motivate and perhaps guide you. A good accountability partner will talk through the five things, see how they went, and maybe ask what you learned from those tasks or what you will do differently. They might ask what you are going to do next to make sure those tasks get the appropriate follow-up.

This might sound intuitive to you, but it's helpful to communicate this information to your accountability partner to make sure you're both on the same page. When I think of the word "partner," I think of someone who is contributing value and interested in the outcome. Your accountability partner needs to know they have permission from you to ask prying questions about your job search and how you are spending your time. It might even make sense to give them a list of questions, like the ones in the previous paragraph, to give them an idea of how open you are to their involvement.

When you start your relationship, also make it clear that you value their input and want them to share their ideas with you. Give them permission to ask deeper questions. With that permission, you need to prepare yourself to have hard conversations about how you spend your time and what tasks you choose to focus on.

This type of open conversation, built on trust and vulnerability, sets you up to have a symbiotic relationship. In a symbiotic relationship both parties benefit. In your case you'll get someone to challenge your ideas and act as a sounding board. The benefit of the motivation you'll get from knowing you are going to report to your partner in a few days cannot be understated. If you're fully open with your partner, you'll also bond deeper with them as they essentially walk with you during one of the hardest times in your life.

Your partner will benefit by increasing their mentoring skills as they tactfully guide you through important thought processes. They will get many opportunities to practice their emotional intelligence, listening skills, probing skills, and other soft skills we all need to practice more. They'll learn more about how to effectively search for a job, which will be helpful in their future job searches. Hopefully they'll get a deeper friendship out of the experience. Finally, many accountability partners will feel good about helping a friend.

The job search can be one of the loneliest experiences of your life. Having someone you can talk to about what you are doing, and bounce ideas off of, can be mentally and emotionally invaluable.

Ending The Partnership

If the person you enlist to be your accountability partner doesn't work out, for whatever reason, don't feel guilty making a change. The ultimate goal is to land the right job for you, and dragging the relationship on will hinder the process.

It's important not to make enemies in the process—how you end the accountability partnership should be clear and respectful. You, or they, might say, "Hey, I realize you were going to be my accountability partner, but this just isn't working for me right now. It's not you, it's not personal, but I'm going to do something different. I really appreciate your willingness to help me. Please let me know if I can be of service to you in any way down the road."

Try to not let terminating the accountability relationship change or tarnish your personal or professional relationship. Learn from the experience and figure out what you can do better with the next accountability partner, and perhaps what changes you should make to the systems you are using or your communication, and move forward. The outcome of getting a job is important, and so is nurturing important relationships.

Even though your first attempt at finding an accountability partner may not lead to a perfect match, it's still essential to make the effort. I wish I had been smart and brave enough to have gotten an accountability partner during my Big Fat Failed Job Search. If I had had an accountability partner, when I applied for job after job without securing interviews, my partner might have helped me realize I needed to change my focus. They might have said, "Jason, you seem to be doing a lot of the right things, but you still aren't getting interviews. We should dig in and see if we can figure out what the problem is." Learn from my mistake and get the right accountability partner to help you be more successful in your job search.

SUMMING IT UP

Creating accountability in your job search is critical. Finding an accountability partner—having someone to report back to—can take your accountability to a whole new level. Your accountability partner should help you stay on track and focus on tasks that actually get you closer to interviews and job offers, such as effective networking, instead of cleaning your email inbox.

The key to a successful accountability program is complete honesty, both with yourself and your accountability partner. Whether you hit your goals or not, just be honest about what you have done. An effective tracking system will help you identify deficiencies in your job search. It will help you see, over time, where you are spending your time and effort so you can decide if you need to make adjustments.

The alternative to this kind of accountability will result in what feels like lots of effort with very little results.

It might make you feel vulnerable to be accountable to yourself and to regularly report to someone else, but trust me, the benefits make that vulnerability worth it!

YOU NEED TO THINK MACRO SO YOU CAN ACT MICRO

In this chapter, I'll discuss how looking at the bigger picture is essential to getting the details right as you search for a job.

SEEING THE BIG PICTURE

I love the book *The 7 Habits of Highly Effective People*[1] by the late Stephen R. Covey—it's one of the best books I've ever read.

Covey's Habit 2 is "begin with the end in mind;" the book explains how highly effective people envision what their end goal is and work backwards from there. It's much easier to figure out the correct path in a maze when I put my pencil on the exit and work backwards towards the entrance. In all aspects of life, we benefit from thinking about where we want to end up and then working backwards.

When you can envision or define the big picture, which includes the end goal, you can make plans and decisions based on the big picture, not just on how you feel today. If you have been on an academic journey, you know the thing that carries you through the difficult instructors, projects, challenges, even politics, is the knowledge that you will receive a certification or degree at the end which will help you achieve your career aspirations in the future. Considering the end game is powerful!

Simon Sinek is famous for his talks, books, and ideas, but perhaps he's most famous for the idea of the importance of finding what he calls your "why."[2] What is your reason for doing what you do? Why are you making significant sacrifices today? A big, important reason motivates us to do the hard things we need to do. This is the "macro" perspective.

Looking at the macro means stepping back and viewing our situation with a high-level perspective instead of hyper-focusing on the immediate problem that is making us want to give up.

Macro is the big picture, the 30,000-foot view, while micro is way down in the woods, looking at the most granular levels.

With regard to your job search, you will be more effective if you take care of, and understand, big picture issues before you aggressively start working on the precise tactics that will get you closer to the job you want. The book *What Color Is Your Parachute?* is another great resource, about knowing where you are headed before you start the job search.[3] It is helpful to ask, "What do I want to be when I grow up?"

As mentioned previously, by the time I started my Big Fat Failed Job Search, I had had three manager/executive titles, none of which were roles I was looking for as a job seeker. I started to look for what I thought I was best suited for: project manager or business analyst jobs. I thought these jobs were right for me because they were closely aligned with my degree and related to what I had been doing the past few years.

One day, while looking at job postings online, I came across a job title I hadn't heard of before. I'd had my head down doing my job, so I wasn't current on other positions the rest of the world knew about. The title was "product manager." The funny thing is that during my early years as a programmer, I had done everything product managers do. I just didn't know that's what it was called. Thankful for this new information, I started focusing my job search on this role, which was more exciting than the other two roles I'd been looking at.

This is a perfect example of going to the macro level in order to be effective at the micro level. Knowing what job I really wanted to pursue helped me focus my time, efforts, and energy.

When you don't have a direction, goal, or target, you are more likely to look at everything and entertain anything. Contrast this to when you know exactly what you are after—

you can be so much more focused and effective!

Imagine you go to the grocery store without a plan. You aren't looking for anything in particular, but you want food that will taste good and bring you comfort. During your shopping spree, you walk through too many aisles, spending too much time in each of them. By the end of your shopping trip, you have a basket full of good tasting regrets which have very little nutritional value and cost an arm and a leg. Contrast that to going to the grocery store with a plan and a list, going straight to the food that is on your list, and getting out of the store quickly, having stayed on budget, and leaving the store with the food you need.

Creating and following a strategy in your job search will help you employ the right tactics, just like it can at the grocery store.

In the 1978 version of *What Color Is Your Parachute?* (the 5th edition), Dick Bolles included the chapters, "Only You Can Decide: What Do You Want to Do?" and "Where Do You Want to Do It?"[4]

Both of those questions are still important today. You are the only person who can decide what you want to do. You need to decide what kind of role you want, or don't want. Define the working conditions, opportunities for growth, culture, etc. that you are interested in. It's critical to have an understanding of what you want so that when you apply to jobs, network, do informational interviews, and craft your brand, you can focus on the right target instead of trying to be all things to all people and applying to every job that comes your way.

Not only do you have to sit down and figure this out, but you *get* to! I know a lot of people who feel stuck in their career or at their organization. Because of various fallacies, including the sunk cost fallacy, they think they've already gone too far down the path to make a change. They have too much expertise, they studied it in school, they are too well-known for it in their industry, etc. to walk away and make a massive career change. I've seen people deep into their career paths, after losing their jobs, question everything. They were in a unique position to rethink what they wanted to do and where they wanted to do it. Some stayed stuck, even though they hated their career, while others chose to make the leap and change directions.

Being in transition is a great time to question everything about your career path. Considering your current or most recent position, are you on a good path with good things to come? Do you make enough money? Are you able to prepare well for retirement? Are you happy?

If you answered "no" to any of those questions, take time to consider what job or career might be better for you. Even if it means doing something you didn't study in school. Even if it means working in an industry or job you never imagined you would work in.

Your transition is a time to reset, so take the time to make sure you are on the right path or identify the path you want to be on.

When you become a job candidate, you become part of the interplay of supply and demand in the hiring market, where candidates like yourself represent supply and employers represent demand. If demand increases for job candidates but supply doesn't change, or if you learn skills that are in high demand, you can get paid more.

As a job candidate it's important to be aware of trends when it comes to demand. What roles are employers struggling to fill? What skills will they pay top dollar for? We call these the market needs.

Your skills, knowledge, abilities, degrees or certifications, network, and experience are what an employer values. These are easier to quantify than soft skills like reliability, being easy to work with, or being drama free, as important as these qualities may be.

There are many things an employer is looking for, and many things you have to offer. The stronger the overlap, the more valuable you are to an employer. If you feel that the job offers you receive aren't what you want, consider looking for a job where the requirements overlap better with your hard skills. Or, if you want to land a job that you don't fully qualify for, do what you need to do to acquire the skills you need.

Here are some macro-level considerations to ponder during this stage in your career:

- What job would I really like to do?
- What do I think would make me happy in my career?
- Do I care about prestige, titles, bragging rights, etc. in my career?
- How much money do I *need* to make (the lowest amount you would say "yes" for)?
- How much money would I *like* to make?
- Do I want to work non-traditional hours?
- How do I feel about working holidays or weekends?
- Do I want to work in a small company or large company?
- What amount of travel am I okay with?
- What are my health insurance requirements?
- What other perks are important/meaningful to me?
- Which perks do I not care about?
- What characteristics in a boss are important to me?
- What characteristics in coworkers are important to me?
- Is continuous training important to me?

As you get a good idea of how you feel about these important questions, you can better identify which companies you should target.

TARGET COMPANIES

During my job search, I heard I should create a target company list, but no one talked about why this was so important. This is more than just making a list of companies that come across your radar, it's making a list of organizations you would love to work for and want to pursue.

So, without understanding how impactful my target company list could be, I started my list by adding companies with openings on job boards and LinkedIn. I even went to business centers in town and figured out what companies were there. I noted the names of the companies listed by the elevators and then went home and researched them.

Frankly, this was a waste of time. I didn't do much with this list except go to the companies' websites and find that no one was hiring, but at least I could say I added more companies to my list (eye roll).

It's important to decide on criteria to use as you learn about organizations and consider if they should make it onto your target company list.

Here are some ideas of what you might include. (Be sure to customize the list to include criteria that are important to *you*!)

Is the company:

- in the right industry for me?
- located in an area where I'm interested in living?
- a company that hires people in my profession?

- in an industry that is growing?
- in an industry that is recession-proof?
- one that is focused on technology?
- a solid blue-chip company?
- a startup?
- a funded startup?
- a funded startup in a hot industry?
- a company where I can put my 9 to 5 in and then walk away every night?
- a company with serious growth potential?
- a company with serious personal growth potential for me?

After my ridiculous attempt to make a target company list by going into buildings and writing down the names of companies in that building, I started to realize a target company list was quite different from a list of companies. Of the 75 or so companies I ultimately wrote down, I was only really interested in 7 to 10 of them. That was my real target company list. Don't make the mistake of thinking a long target company list is the goal. It's okay if your target company list for the duration of your job search only includes five companies.

If a company comes across your radar that doesn't meet the criteria to make it onto your list, you don't have to ignore it. Maybe what you learn about the organization or the opportunity sounds too good to pass up or work towards—it's okay to include it on the list. But when it comes to figuring out where to focus your resources, use your criteria and target company list as a general guide.

SHARPEN YOUR SAW . . . ER, AXE

Abraham Lincoln is attributed as saying:

> "Give me six hours to chop down a tree and I will spend the first four sharpening the axe."

Stephen Covey's Habit 7 from *The 7 Habits of Highly Effective People* is "sharpen the saw."[5] Thinking at the macro level to act at the micro level is all about getting clarity and direction. This involves doing exercises to redefine who you are and what you want. It's about laying a foundation and creating a vision.

Completing these self-awareness exercises, and exercises you'll find in college career centers (have you tapped into your alumni college career center yet?), will be an invaluable investment into your job search. It might not feel like you are doing enough, but just as Abe Lincoln supposedly alluded to, you need to spend a significant amount of time and thought preparing, which will make the rest of your job search much better.

CHANGES AND FOCUS

One final note: Make sure you allow for change and flexibility. It's okay if you decide to change your big picture, your objectives, your "why." And it's also okay to change directions in your career. What you thought you'd do when you grew up has probably changed over the years. When I was young, it went from either getting rich or working with animals to having some kind of executive job. As I settled into the workforce, I learned that maybe working at a smaller company wasn't so bad and I could really enjoy it.

When I started my Big Fat Failed Job Search, I was focused on getting a job, but within a couple of months, I'd changed courses and was spending a lot of time getting my own business up and running. I became an entrepreneur, not by choice, rather because of circumstances and opportunities, and I have changed who I am and where I'm going. This journey has been everchanging, not because I'm fickle, but because outside influences changed. My income needs changed as my family grew, opportunities changed as the economy changed, and demands on my time changed. Even with, and perhaps because of, these changes, I'm very happy with where my career is at. I've loved most aspects of being an entrepreneur.

My tactics, the things I spent time doing, changed as I changed my focus. Once I identified where I wanted to end up, I was able to spend my time where I needed to, not where others said I should. All of my efforts were directed at getting me to that end result.

One of the beautiful things about a transition period is that you finally can take the time to pause, breathe, and ask yourself some hard questions. This is the time to look at the big picture. This is the time to initiate the career conversations you may have been avoiding for a long time. If you find yourself indecisive or wishy-washy, that's okay! Give yourself some space as you try to figure out what you want and need.

Be honest with yourself, especially about yourself. Find people you can talk to about the big picture. Sometimes getting insight and perspective from others can really help you get grounded. It's easy to get so caught up in what we think is right, what we think we need to do, that we can focus on those things so much that we miss out on opportunities we should pursue.

Don't beat yourself up if you aren't where you wanted to be by now. Don't worry if you worked hard to achieve something and it turned out the dream was better than the reality. Maturity in your career means taking the information you have right now, combined with your values and desires, and charting a new course that will give you the best outcome possible. There's no shame in changing the path you are on. Just make sure you are on a path you want to be on, and making progress, even if that means you are spending time at the 30,000-foot level for a time. Going back to the quote attributed to Lincoln, spend 66% of your time preparing and the other 33% being as effective as possible.

SUMMING IT UP

Now is an excellent time to step back from the daily grind and "begin with the end in mind," as Stephen Covey recommends—envision how you want your future to play out. When you have an idea of what you want for your career now, and how you want to end your career, you can make a plan and work towards that vision. This includes understanding your motivations, or your "why," as Simon Sinek puts it. Ask yourself Dick Bolles' questions: "What do you want to do?" and "Where do you want to do it?"

Take advantage of this transition to rethink your career and the direction you are heading. Ask yourself the hard questions you find in this chapter. Once you have a better idea of what you want, what your vision is, and what your "why" is, identify and network into organizations that align with what you want. Invest time in yourself and be okay with changes to how you feel and what you think you want as you work through this time in your career.

NOTES

---

[1] Stephen R. Covey. *The 7 Habits of Highly Effective People: Powerful Lessons in Personal Change.* New York: Simon & Schuster, 2013.

[2] TEDx Talks. "Start with Why—How Great Leaders Inspire Action. Simon Sinek, TEDxPugetSound." September 28, 2009. Video. https://www.youtube.com/watch?v=u4ZoJKF_VuA.

[3] Richard N. Bolles. *What Color Is Your Parachute?: Your Guide to a Lifetime of Meaningful Work and Career Success.* New York: Ten Speed Press, 2022.

[4] Richard N. Bolles. *What Color Is Your Parachute?: A Practical Manual for Job Hunters & Career Changers.* Berkeley: Ten Speed Press, 1978.

[5] Covey, *The 7 Habits of Highly Effective People.*

YOU NEED TO TAKE CARE OF YOURSELF

A difficult job search can be all-encompassing and overwhelming to the point that many job searchers neglect their health and relationships. I know when I switched from being the sole breadwinner to being unemployed, I felt like a third-class citizen and that every bit of effort and drive I could muster up needed to be invested into landing my next job.

I wanted to land a job with a salary that was at least as high as my previous salary, and preferably something that felt like a step up in my career, and I knew doing so would require a lot of hard work. One of the results of working hard on my job search was that I neglected my physical, spiritual, and mental health and neglected my relationships.

WHY TAKE CARE OF YOURSELF?

I fully understand the urgency of getting a salary coming in again. I understand the anxiety and all the other feelings and emotions. But if no one else has told you this, let me be the first to tell you—despite the desire to throw 100% of yourself into your job search, you have to take care of yourself.

How can you afford to take the time necessary to take care of yourself? The real question is, how can you afford *not* to? Taking care of yourself is absolutely essential to performing your best during your job search. Maybe you can neglect yourself for a few days and be okay, but please, please don't neglect yourself for weeks, which can lead to months, which can lead to years.

When I started my job search, my dad kindly said, "I'll expect you to be out of work for at least six months." Six months? Did he have me mixed up with someone else? I was the ambitious one, the one who got things done, the one who had proven I have drive. I was the one who chose a career in tech which I assumed meant I would never be out of work for very long. I fully expected to be sitting at a desk with a comfortable salary within three months! But the more I networked, the more I learned that people like me, people who were looking for jobs like those I was looking for, were not landing jobs in weeks—they were landing jobs after months and months.

I have heard career professionals say you can expect a job search to last one month for every $10,000 you want to make. If you are targeting $70,000, expect to take seven months in your job search. Looking for jobs that pay $120,000? Expect to be out of work for 12 months.

This process of looking for a job while wondering how you are going to pay the bills or buy food when the money runs out in a few months is scary.

When I think about doing really hard things, I think about a time when I was 14. I swam to the bottom of a pool, probably to get something, and as I was swimming up, I could see the surface a foot or two away and my lungs felt like they were going to burst. It was so hard! I wasn't sure I would actually make it.

Of course, I did make it. The human resolve is very strong. But that feeling of being at the very end of my capabilities is one I go back to when I have to do something hard. I remind myself that I can hold my breath for a bit and endure hardship or pain. And I remind myself that when it passes, I will take a deep breath and feel safe again.

Sometimes we go into a job search thinking we'll sacrifice everything for the short time it takes to get to the surface. We have a singular focus: survival. Because of that singular focus, nothing else matters, and that's how we start to neglect things.

Another reason to take care of yourself during your job search is so that when you land a job, you can bring a healthy you to your next role. Interestingly, the first hurt and brokenness you feel in your job search has a lot to do with second-guessing yourself and wondering why you are unemployed. But after months of neglect, you become more hurt or broken. Avoid that by strategically and purposefully doing things to take care of yourself.

The harder this job search is, the longer it is, the more likely it will change you forever. I have talked to plenty of people who you would imagine have it all together and have amazing careers. But when you start talking about layoffs, being unemployed, and all the things someone typically goes through during a difficult job search, you can see signs of PTSD.

Please recognize the reality of the incredibly difficult time you are going through. Respect this reality. And make sure you fight to maintain or strengthen your physical, spiritual, mental, and relationship health.

TAKE CARE OF YOUR RELATIONSHIPS

It may not seem like a big deal to ignore your spouse, kids, or other significant people in your life for a couple of days in order to hyperfocus on your job search (finding a new job is important and necessary after all!). But if you get into the habit of neglecting your relationships, and your job search goes longer than expected, the days of neglect could turn into weeks, and before you even realize what has happened, you have neglected your relationships for months. Trust me, I know from personal experience! If you fail to nurture your important relationships during your job search, it might be something you don't recover from, ever.

During my job search, I heard about a conversation my wife had had a few months earlier. She was chatting with a friend who asked how I was doing. That's what sometimes happens during a job search . . . people ask others how you are doing instead of asking you how you are doing. I think this happens because job seekers seem hurt, and people want to be positive instead of wallowing in misery with the job seeker.

Anyway, my wife's friend asked her how I was doing, and my wife replied, "I don't know, we don't talk anymore."

Hearing this broke my heart. I realized that, indeed, we didn't talk about hardly anything anymore. It's as if we had a pact that I would only share good news with her and she would only share good news with me. We were in emotional survival mode and didn't want to bring one another down with our worries.

How do you think only talking when there was something positive to share worked out? Well, since there rarely was anything positive, we rarely spoke. Yes, of course, we talked about the logistical things we needed to talk about, but not much more. While we were trying to be strong for each other, our relationship suffered.

I'm sad that I did that to my wife. She needed a husband, whether I was employed or not. Our relationship needed to be fed, not starved. Jeopardizing the health of my most important relationships is one of my biggest regrets. And it took years to recover from that neglect.

Please continue to love on your loved ones even while you feel hurt, broken, or incomplete. Investing in your important relationships will pay off for many decades to come. Bonus: The benefits that come from having great relationships will bring a healthier you to your job search.

PROTECT YOUR PHYSICAL HEALTH

Protecting your physical health is the first thing people often think of when they think of taking care of themselves. If you are a gym rat but you have to discontinue your membership while you are without an income, figure out other ways to create a challenging workout. There are plenty of free workout videos on YouTube, and many other free resources such as podcasts, exercise plans, blog posts, articles, etc. to help you create a home workout. To work out, all you really need is gravity, which I'm guessing you have in abundance where you live.

One of the things that saved me during my job search, and then as I started a business and worked from home (which felt like a job search—lots of work but no money coming in!), was walking. I figured out a one-mile loop I could walk in my neighborhood, and then later, a three-mile loop. Over the years I've figured out other things I could do from the comfort of my home, like push-ups against the wall or on the stairs, yoga, etc.

There are a lot of newfangled ideas about physical fitness. The bottom line is that you need to move. Move for cardio or move for weight resistance. Move to stretch or move for balance. But move. Get up, get out, and move.

Another important factor in your physical health is nutrition. Be careful what you eat. Make sure you eat plenty of fruits, vegetables, and other whole foods. Take in less sugar. Drink more water. All that stuff you already know. I don't mean to sound cliche, but this is serious stuff.

I love me some pizza, donuts, chocolate, fries, and soda. But I have learned, especially as I've aged and my body doesn't handle food like it did when I was a teenager, that what we put in our mouths is a big part of taking care of our bodies. The phrase that has stuck with me is, "If you take care of your body, it will take care of you."[1]

When you are undergoing a job search, you need to avoid the lows that come with sugar crashes, or sleepless nights because you chose to eat a horrible (but tasty) meal. I'm not saying you have to go on a super clean diet, rather, that you need to be intentional about your physical health and how you fuel your body, and pay attention to the consequences of your food choices.

Finally, make sure you are getting proper sleep. Once, when I had begged my way into a job interview (I didn't have many interviews in my job search), I didn't do what I needed to in order to sleep well the night before. Guess how that interview went? Not well! The interviewer was gracious, but I was not at my best, simply because I had neglected, even abused, my physical health.

There are plenty of hacks to help you sleep better, from adjusting the temperature of your room to tweaking when and what you eat and other environmental factors. Practicing mindfulness and making your bedroom a more peaceful place can also help you sleep better. Your body, and your brain, need the rest that a good, deep sleep can provide. Not sleeping well takes a toll on your physical and mental health, so be intentional about sleep. If you have sleep problems, do some research and try out the various suggestions until you find out what works for you.

You never know when you are going to get your big chance and be in front of the right people, the people who could make a huge difference in your life—sometimes you'll land an unexpected job interview or, at the last minute, you'll learn about a networking event. Maybe you just need to be mentally there for an important follow-up email you are writing. If you neglect your health, you may write a subpar email, and being subpar is not a luxury serious job seekers get to enjoy.

PROTECT YOUR SPIRITUAL AND MENTAL HEALTH

Thank goodness that over the last few years, society has really embraced the idea of taking care of our spiritual and mental health. Now, during this difficult phase of your career, you need to protect your spiritual and mental health like your life depends upon it. Because, well, maybe it does.

Spiritual Health

Because spirituality means different things to different people, I don't know exactly what will most help you, but consider what helps you feel connected to God or your higher power or the universe. Whether you connect with the spiritual through being in nature or meditating, or you attend church or pray, make sure you do what you need to do to nurture a spiritual connection.

When you take time to be still and ponder eternity and the grand scheme of things, you will have more peace and be more confident in making the important decisions you need to make during your job search. Taking care of your spiritual health will also help you perform better during your job search, and as an added bonus, it will have a positive impact on other aspects of your health.

Mental Health

My Big Fat Failed Job Search began in January of 2006. That March was when I had the idea to create JibberJobber, which launched on May 15th. Two really interesting things happened because of JibberJobber that raised my mental health awareness.

First, once I started working on JibberJobber, I couldn't sleep past four or five in the morning, and I'm NOT a morning person. But my brain would start going and my eyes would pop open, ready to work. I was running on adrenaline and couldn't rest. It was so exciting and so refreshing to be out of the dark drudgery of a job search that was producing zero results and being able to be productive and have meaningful work to do. It was exciting to the point that it kept me up at night.

What I learned is that when I had something to work on that I was interested in and passionate about, it gave me hope, and everything changed. I was happier. I could breathe again. I could even smile again. It was my "JibberJobber moment." That's what I call the turning point where you go from dark to light, from depressed to full of hope.

Now, I'm not saying you need to figure out how to start your own business. I fully recognize that many people would be miserable as entrepreneurs. But I do want you to figure out what your JibberJobber moment might be.

My JibberJobber moment was when I came up with this crazy idea to create a CRM for job seekers. Your Jibber-Jobber moment might be when you finally decide to look into a career change and start to do something you can be more passionate about. Isn't that an exciting idea?

I'm talking about figuring out something that gives you hope. For the longest time, I honestly didn't understand what hope was or how important it is. Once I spent time thinking about it, I came up with the phrase, "I didn't understand what hope was until I had lost it."

Before I lost my job, I think I naturally had some kind of hope, some optimistic vision. But when I lost my job, I lost more than a salary, benefits, vacation time, and the security and pride that comes with a title and working for a cool company—I lost my identity, and perhaps most detrimental of all, I lost hope. Not the day I got laid off, but over the next few weeks as I came to realize my job search was going to be long and hard.

And then I found myself up by 5:00 am, working on this idea that was going to change the world. I said dark to light a few sentences ago, but really, it was like going from a black-and-white show to a show with the most vivid colors you can imagine.

I realize mental health is more than having hope. Sometimes you need therapy with a skillful, licensed professional. Sometimes you need medication. If you might need those things, please seek them out!

In addition, make an effort to learn about how to improve aspects of your mental health. If the job search is a stimulus that impacts your mental health negatively, maybe there are some easy things you can do, other stimuli you can introduce, that will impact your mental health positively. Don't underestimate how much your diet and exercise (or lack of exercise) can affect your mood. Don't discount the power of vitamins and minerals, especially vitamin D. Spend time in nature, even if that simply means hanging out in your backyard or at a local park. Meditate. Learn about the vagus nerve. Notice what things trigger you during difficult situations, and be curious about why you are triggered. Make an effort to breathe and stay calm. Make sure you don't indulge in harmful habits, rather, create new habits with healthy coping skills.

Neglecting your spiritual and mental health can drag your job search on and allow depression to spiral. I know, I've been there. I have seen it in many other job seekers I've worked with. This is something you absolutely want to do with intention and purpose.

SUMMING IT UP

There are hundreds of thousands of books on all aspects of health and relationships on Amazon. There are all kinds of angles, philosophies, systems, programs, testimonials, etc. Find resources that resonate with and help you. I am asking, even begging, you to take the time necessary to take care of yourself and your relationships.

More than one job seeker I've spoken to has told me that during their job search, they finally made the time to begin taking care of themselves and got into the best shape they'd been in for a long time. Being heads-down at your job for your entire working life can be exhausting. Some job seekers find the job search a time to take a break from the hectic rat race, and finally get their health back in order. This is a great opportunity for you. Whether you do it so you can be more on your game now or so you can enjoy better health for years to come, it doesn't matter. What does matter is that you are intentional about how you take care of yourself.

NOTES

---

[1] Ted Lindsay. Quoted in Michelle Winfrey, *Lose Weight Fast and Now: 365+ Motivating Quotes On Losing Weight, On Diet, on Fitness.* Independently published, 2020.

YOU NEED TO MASTER THE INTERVIEW PROCESS

During my Big Fat Failed Job Search, I attended a great job search seminar where we talked about how to ace an interview. It was fun, interesting, strategic, and tactical. One of the most impactful things we did was a mock interview, which I'll discuss later in this chapter. By the end of the multi-day seminar, I felt empowered and was excited for future interviews!

After attending that interview seminar, I had a pretty good handle on what an effective interview should look like. And I was appalled at the job interviews I was part of as I tried to land a job—they were unprofessional and seemed to be unplanned.

The interviewers asked me generic questions that they read from a sheet of paper. Questions I would have never asked someone interviewing for that job. Some of the cutesy, cliche questions they asked me were garbage. Even though I was interviewing for a software manager job, they asked me the same questions I would have expected if I had been looking for a fast food job. It seemed as though the interviewer printed "top 100 interview questions" and picked up the hot-off-the press printout on the way to the interview without thinking about which questions were relevant!

I'll never forget the interview I was perhaps most excited about. It was for a project manager job at an up-and-coming hardware company. I had an excellent interview with the hiring manager and then was asked if I had time to talk with the two project managers already on the team. The project managers asked me a few questions and then, when I asked them a question, one of them said, "Honestly, we didn't even know there was an opening, so we are surprised to even be here right now."

I didn't know if it was an LOL moment or an Oh Crap moment, but I figured if they didn't know about the job, something fishy was up. I was crushed when, a few days later, I received a generic rejection email. But I couldn't help thinking the manager was probably toxic and perhaps I was saved from a horrible work environment.

PREPARING FOR AN INTERVIEW

Humans are funny beasts. The funny, even dysfunctional part of us reveals itself in the job search process. Our quirks, and the quirks of those involved in a hiring decision, can unfairly or illogically impact any part of the hiring process. Some interviews are overly formal and impersonal and the interviewer treats you like a number instead of a person. It's as if the interviewer is indifferent about asking you the same questions they've already asked dozens of other candidates.

By no means am I saying we need to remove humans and automate job interviews. I'm just recognizing that yes, just about every part of the job search is imperfect, and no, many problems are unlikely to be resolved, especially on a global level. While every interview will be different, and not all interviewers are going to do a great job, there are some things you can do to prepare to have the best interview possible.

The most important thing to understand is what, from the perspective of the interviewer, is the purpose of the interview. Of course, there isn't a one-size-fits-all answer—that would make things too easy. Sometimes, the purpose of the interview is to create a small pool of qualified candidates. Sometimes, the interview is a formality required by law or policy, even though the organization has already decided who they will hire. Sometimes the purpose is to find someone to hire who is the right technical fit, other times it's to find a person with the right cultural or team fit.

The best way to understand the purpose of the interview is to contact an insider at the organization, someone you may have met through networking, to ask more about the opportunity. Someone on the inside might be able to tell you what the interviewers are looking for, how the interviews are going, and what the competition looks like.

Also, prior to your interview, do as much research as you can about the organization, opportunity, people on the team you are interviewing for, and even market trends that might uncover what the company's competitors are doing.

During the interview, pay attention to each question, and how the questions are asked. You might find a certain theme that dominates the interview, which likely tells you that area is a problem they need help solving. Questions about how you handle problems might give you insight into what you need to do to be successful in the role. Use this information to craft questions for the interviewers and then pay attention to how they respond.

When you are asked a question, one of the things you need to ask yourself is, "Why are they asking me this question?" Although some questions will feel generic, recently printed, without much thought, other questions might have a purpose to them.

You want to figure out that purpose. It might be to get an idea of your technical proficiency or to assess how well you will fit into the team. Questions might be posed to see how fast you think on your feet, to see if you have had certain experiences important to your role, or to see how you act when you are frustrated or don't know an answer.

When you understand the purpose of an interview and the intent of an interviewer's question, you can answer in a way that addresses that intent. The employer uses resumes to screen candidates and figure out which ones should get interviews, and then in the interview, they try to figure out if the candidates can actually do the job. They're trying to figure out if you have the experience, training, credentials, or some other quantifiable skill that shows you have done or can do this job. Maybe you have done similar tasks and will be trainable, or able to easily come up to speed. Questions to get to the heart of this include experiential questions like, "Tell me about a time you had to. . . ."

Interviewers also ask questions to help them determine whether you will be a good addition to the team. This is often described as "fit," for example cultural fit or team fit. Some people think considering fit is superficial or unimportant. I think it's critical, and I guarantee if humans are involved in an interview, they are assessing for fit, even if they don't know it.

From the very first contact until the very last contact, people will be observing you and trying to determine whether you will be a good addition to the team or not. There are legendary stories of the person who didn't get a job because they were rude to the receptionist. I heard of a hiring manager who posed as the receptionist to get first-hand information on how the candidates would treat someone of a perceived lesser role.

I've heard stories about an employer observing the parking area to identify the car of an applicant, then looking through the windows to see if their car was tidy or a cluttered mess.

It doesn't sound fair, I know, but again, when humans are involved, not everything will be fair. People will watch how you interact with others in the room. They'll look for any indications of what you think is appropriate, your language, your vocabulary, everything.

When you leave, they'll talk about you. Whether it was one person with you who talks with colleagues, other managers, or their boss, or it was a panel interview, people will talk. You'll be remembered simply as the person with the cool resume, the person who worked at that one company, the person who had an unusual handshake, or the person who was really impressive and polished.

I don't mean to make you paranoid, but it pays to prepare, be aware of how a prospective employer might perceive you both within and outside of the interview, and then relax and have a good conversation. The interviewer may be nervous too, but if you're able to relax, it will help them relax as well. Of course, you have a lot riding on it, but at the end of the day, a job interview ideally would be approached like any other business meeting—you'll have better results if you're able to be at ease.

In addition to taking care of yourself by eating well, getting the rest you need before an interview, and possibly getting up a little early to get some exercise, it's a good idea to get to an interview location early to avoid the stress of being in a rush and the potential of being late. Would you rather be 30 minutes early and sit in your car or at a nearby park than be 30 minutes late because of heavy traffic and miss the opportunity? Providing a cushion in your travel time will help your mind be in a good, healthy place during the interview.

An interviewer allots a certain amount of time for your interview. While you might have all day free, and would love to extend the conversation over lunch and then get a tour of the building, they might have a booked calendar, even meeting with a dozen other candidates that day. Every second you get in the interview is important.

Years ago, after I wrote my first book about LinkedIn, I was invited to do some radio interviews. I had done other types of interviews, mostly print and podcast interviews, but this was the first time I was going to be on live radio. The person scheduling me asked if I had ever done radio before and I said "no." She told me the most important thing to remember was that I only had a few seconds to respond to questions. They wanted me to respond to question after question in quick succession. The scheduler stressed that if I talked too long, listeners would get bored and change the station.

This was really interesting advice, advice I needed to hear because I tend to be long-winded. During a job interview, response length is also important to consider. You don't want to go on and on to the point that your interviewer is dozing in their chair or counting the seconds until they can move on to interviewing the next candidate. Rather, be focused and deliberate as you respond.

ANSWERING INTERVIEW QUESTIONS WITH MINI-STORIES

As you respond to interview questions, tie your response into the specific role you are interviewing for. For example, if the interviewer asks you an experiential question for a product manager role like, "Tell me about a time you have had to deal with a team that just doesn't get along," you can talk about an experience where you helped a team get along better and be more productive, and then say something like, "As a product manager I think bringing people together is one of the most important soft skills. In addition to the example I just shared, I've had other opportunities to do this in my career and am known by my colleagues as someone who contributes to a cohesive team." Isn't that beautiful? You are tying your past experiences into what you hope to be your next role: the product manager at their organization.

At a job club I went to, they emphasized the importance of responding to almost any interview question with a formula that I call a mini-story. The formula is similar to the age-old PAR statement: Problem, Action, Results. Enhancing your PAR statement to become a mini-story will help you as a job seeker and will also help your personal brand.

Stories are powerful because they are more memorable than, say, statistics. Because stories connect on an emotional level, if you incorporate mini-stories, your interview will be more memorable than those of interviewees who didn't have the emotional connection that comes through sharing stories. Here's an example response using the mini-story method to answer the question, "Tell me about a time you have had to deal with a team that just doesn't get along."

A. **State that you have the skill or characteristic they are looking for:** "I am known as someone who is good at bringing troubled teams together."

B. **Action (tell a story, give an example):** "In my previous job I was assigned to a team that was continually running behind and frustrated. Management was struggling to deal with the team's problems because each person on the team was needed but emotions were high. After a couple of weeks of being on the team, I realized we needed to make three changes: A, B, and C."

C. **Now, tell the results:** "After we made those changes, our team turned out to be the tightest, highest performing team in our division. It was really awesome to be involved in bringing that team together. I'd be happy to introduce you to my boss, who can tell you more about that experience."

Isn't that powerful? You are basically saying: "I am proficient in this. I have dealt with this before and was able to achieve the results my organization needed."

Now, let's take the mini-story method to the next level to make them even more powerful! A few years ago, I spoke to a career adviser in Dallas, Texas. She was a charming lady who had spent decades helping people from all walks of life move from unemployed and frustrated to landing real, life-changing jobs. We were talking about the power of these mini-stories and she said, "Jason, there's one more part to this. You have to tell the interviewer *why* your mini-story is important to them!"

This impacted me so heavily! Of course! Previously, I'd been focusing on responding to interviewers' questions with "A, then B, then C." But she opened my eyes to the importance of decreasing an interviewer's mental load by doing the heavy lifting for them and helping them come to the conclusion you would like them to. In addition to telling them "I'm awesome and here's what I did," you go a step further by saying, "and I can do this for you at your company!"

The "I can do this at your company" is the D to the A, B, and C. It completes your statement. It makes for a stronger argument. It makes you stand out as more than just a competent candidate, but the best candidate right now for this role at their company.

Note that you can use mini-stories outside of interviews. Have a networking lunch? It might be highly appropriate to share one of your mini-stories. You can use mini-stories in your LinkedIn profile, on your personal website, and in other places. Add these powerful mini-stories to your list of marketing assets that help you really quantify and communicate who you are and what value you bring to a prospective employer.

THE EMBARRASSING MOCK INTERVIEW

I was going to write "The Powerful Mock Interview" but my fingers typed "embarrassing" automatically before I could stop them. I was sick-to-my-stomach nervous when I first participated in a mock interview. It felt so fake and contrived, but it was such an enriching, helpful experience.

My mock interview experience took place with a mentor and about five other job seekers during the course of a multi-day seminar. The interview room was set up with a camera that recorded us. One of us pretended we were the interviewer while another practiced answering questions. The rest of the group watched through a two-way mirror.

I think we all went into our interviews thinking we were pretty good at interviewing. We were seasoned professionals. We all had experience interviewing job seekers. I was shocked to see how every single person choked during their first mock interview.

We expected polished responses from each other. What we saw instead was a lot of, er . . . um . . . filler words. We saw fuddled responses that made the interviewee sound unsure

107

of themselves. Every single person left that interview room feeling embarrassed. More importantly, we left realizing we needed to prepare and practice. Better we mess up in a mock interview than during the real thing. Build muscle memory by going through the questions you know you are going to be asked, like, "Tell me about yourself," and questions that are common for the role you are interviewing for.

One of the best ways to practice interviewing is to do actual interviews as often as you can—do what you can to land as many interviews as possible. Each interview will allow you to practice your introduction, mini-stories, sharing parts of your personal brand, and relaxing and communicating naturally so you're even better prepared for your next interview. Doing mock interviews will also help you practice these important skills. If you aren't interviewing with real employers, practice your interviewing skills by doing mock interviews. Whether you do this just once, or you do this regularly, even before every real interview you do, your interviewing skills will improve!

Our mock interview setup may sound complicated, but you don't need to have an elaborate setup to do mock interviews. Don't have a special room with a two-way mirror? No problem—any room should do. Don't have a group of friends you can, or want to, practice with? That's fine—all you really need is one person, or you can even practice with yourself.

You can write out your answers and wordsmith them until you feel really comfortable with them. Memorize them, not to spout them off and sound robotic, but to build muscle memory. We have this idea that memorizing answers will make us sound canned. If you memorize answers and then practice them, with an effort to answer in a relaxed and natural way, you can come up with much better responses.

I have seen this in the job search, and I've seen it with my own work creating courses and presentations. Years ago, when I started creating courses for Pluralsight, I didn't script my courses—I thought I was good enough to just go off the cuff and create great content. I received great ratings and a lot of people watched my courses. But eventually I realized I could improve my courses by scripting them. I now rework my script at least six times before recording. Relistening to my old courses, it's clear that they are so much better now that I script them! If you fail to prepare and practice, you might wonder for years how your life could have been different. If you prepare for an important interview by practicing, you won't regret it.

A DIFFICULT QUESTION

In addition to preparing for the questions you are excited to respond to, the questions that will show you are indeed the best hire for the job, you need to prepare and practice a response for one of the harder, more uncomfortable questions. The question I'm referring to is, "Why did you leave your last job?"

In answering this question, I've found that a lot of people are embarrassed and feel the need to defend their honor and make sure the interviewer knows they aren't the broken person they assume the interviewer thinks they are.

When answering the questions, "What happened? Why don't you have a job?" you may struggle to follow the counsel, "If you don't have anything nice to say, don't say anything at all." Maybe your boss was a total jerk. Maybe the work environment was toxic, or you got burned out from everchanging goals. Maybe your coworkers were unsafe. Or maybe you were underappreciated or misunderstood and you were fired, or your company had to downsize and most of your department was laid off.

Whatever your reason for being unemployed, sharing all your thoughts and feelings about what happened might do more harm than good. Telling interviewers that your last boss was a jerk or your coworkers were lazy slobs might get a chuckle, but in the back of their minds, they will likely wonder if you were the problem or if you will talk about them that way. Either way, focusing the blame on your former colleagues will have negative consequences.

Figure out how to tactfully answer the question. People don't need the backstory, nor do they need all the juicy details. Think of the question as a test by the interviewer to determine if they will like working with you. Some reasonable reasons for leaving a previous job are that you wanted better career opportunities, were looking for growth opportunities, or needed a better work-life balance. Notice how you can easily answer this question without saying anything about the work environment.

Of course, people want honest colleagues, but you can honestly sum up what they need to know in a sentence or two, with no drama or dirt. Figure out what your statement is, practice it, and leave the drama for the appropriate place and time.

YOUR QUESTIONS ARE JUST AS IMPORTANT AS THEIRS

One of the most important things you should do in your interview preparation is create a list of questions for you to ask the interviewer if you have the opportunity. This opportunity usually arises towards the end of an interview. Remember what I said about understanding the intent of the questions an interviewer asks you? Think about the intent of your questions and what the interviewer might perceive the intent of your questions to be.

An interview is a two-way evaluation. As the interviewer is evaluating you, you're also evaluating them as a potential future employer. I remember being at the end of my financial runway, wondering how I was going to buy food or pay my bills. If I'd have had a chance to get a paycheck and get back into society, I'd have jumped on it. But what if I were to have gotten bad vibes during an interview?

Should you take a job if you see red flags? Imagine you are in an interview and you learn the job you applied for is different than what you thought. What if you thought it required only a little bit of travel, but you learn they want you to be on the road 50% of the time? What if you learn they want you to work in a different location than you assumed, and you're not comfortable with the commute distance? What if the people interviewing you seem a little off, even unenthusiastic about the role you are interviewing for? I've been in a few interviews where some of the interviewers seemed bored during the interview. It's common for managers to bring in team members to an interview, even though they shouldn't really be there. I remember one interview, alluded to earlier in this chapter, where two of my would-be colleagues were asking me questions about the role because they didn't even know there was an opening on their small team. I think they were worried about their own future at the organization! What should you do if your gut is telling you this boss, or this team, is going to be a really bad fit?

This is a complex topic. I can't tell you that you should, or shouldn't, take a job. A lot of people have this erroneous idea that job seekers need to get over themselves and take any job they can land, even if it's an entry-level fast food job, so they can make money while looking for their next career job, but for many people, that is an unrealistic and unfair expectation.

This is a common problem professionals in transition face. People who haven't been in their position think they are "too good" to do any work, that some work is below them, etc. I know a lot of professionals who would take a hit to their ego serving up fries. But the idea that a person should take any job while in transition is a problem much bigger than having a big ego. It's hard to stay focused and do everything you need to do in a higher-level job search when you are busy putting hours in, and getting exhausted at another job that isn't right for you.

But saying "yes" to a job that isn't ideal to help pay your bills and keep you afloat for a while longer might be the right thing to do. If you do this, go into it knowing that your job search is not over and you'll spend time looking for a better opportunity while working at that job.

There's power in knowing you have options, even if while working at that job you'll need to keep looking. The alternative, which might be getting evicted or not paying your bills, could be devastating.

I know that job seekers sometimes feel desperate, and it can seem reckless to be selective in choosing a job. But if you have the financial flexibility, it's okay to be selective and look at the entire interview experience to determine whether you want to work for this organization or not.

Just as you are probably on your best behavior during an interview, the interviewer should be on their best behavior. If what you see isn't that impressive, imagine what it will be like once you are hired. I'm not saying it will always be downhill from there, but take this into consideration as you ask an interviewer questions and evaluate if their organization is one you would want to spend a big chunk of your day working for.

One of the first things I advise people, with regard to questions to ask the interviewer, is to avoid all simple questions you can answer yourself with a little research. "Where is your headquarters?" "Who founded the company?" "How big is your company?" and similar questions can usually be answered by looking at an organization's website, searching on Google, or using LinkedIn or Crunchbase.

Speaking of which, did you know you can sometimes access expensive research databases with an account at your local library? It's worth a visit to the library to see what resources you can tap into.

Back to the questions you ask in an interview. . . . In formulating your questions, consider the following two objectives:

1. To learn something.
2. To stand out as an excellent candidate.

Also, consider the timing of your questions. Some experts say that during the first interview, you shouldn't ask about raises, vacation time, insurance, or other perks that make it look like you are only interested in what the organization is going to give to you. The people who make that argument basically say this interview is a time to really sell yourself, and you should not let anything distract from the idea that you are the best candidate.

I have a difficult time with this advice because information about benefits and perks is important information that will help you weigh this opportunity against other opportunities before you invest too much time in pursuing it. Also, asking questions about these things shows you are detail-oriented and are able to consider a much bigger picture and not just be influenced by a salary amount. I recommend you read the room. If you feel like an offer may be coming your way, the first interview might be a great time to talk about some of those details.

Ask questions as if you had the role—"assume the sale." For example:

> "What does success in this role look like during the first 90 days?"

This question shows that not only do you think you can do this job (showing confidence in your proficiency), but you want to make sure you do it well, contributing to the success of your team, your boss, and the organization.

Another type of question might get to the heart of their organization's culture. You could ask about flexible work schedules or continuing learning and growth opportunities. These questions will give you a good idea of how the organization values and invests in their employees. If you love working remotely, or at least want the flexibility, make sure you ask if that option is available.

You'll find plenty of examples of questions to ask during your interview through an online search. Look for questions that are relevant to your role and level, and remember to consider the intent, and perceived intent, of each question you ask.

The interview process, which might include multiple interviews with different people, should help you get a good idea of the overall opportunity. Can you do the work? Will you like the work and are the deadlines reasonable? Are the boss and colleagues people you want to spend time with? Will you be fairly compensated? Does the organization value the employee and their life outside of the office? How are they investing in their employees and creating a work environment that people want to stay in?

I used to think salary was the key criteria for deciding where to work. But through experiences over the years in a variety of organizations, I've learned there is a lot more to my happiness in and out of work than just the paycheck. That might sound elitist, but I've seen people who make what they think they are worth, sometimes even a lot more, who are miserable.

As you ask questions during an interview, you're able to assess the company and determine if you would enjoy working there.

FOLLOW UP

We talked about the importance of following up when you network. Following up after a job interview is equally important.

A while back, I needed to interview about a dozen people for a job opening I was hiring for, and to be honest, after about the fourth candidate, I began to forget who had said what. Yes, I took notes, but it was too easy to forget which applicants I liked and which impressed me.

Remember the idea I shared from Keith Ferrazzi—If you want to be better than 95% of your competition, all you have to do is follow up?[1] When you're interviewing for a job, you definitely want to be better than the competition!

Sometimes following up feels old fashioned. Do people really send thank you cards anymore? Seriously, isn't sending a text or email sufficient? Yes, it can be. Based on my own experience as a hiring manager, even a text or email is more than what most people do. But do you want just "sufficient," or do you want to go above and beyond to ensure you are remembered?

On their blog and in their book, *Guerrilla Marketing for Job Hunters 3.0*, Jay Levinson and my friend Dave Perry provide lots of great follow-up tips to help you stand out as a job seeker.[2] For example, after an interview, you could send the employer a coffee cup or box of donuts. You can find other great tips from Jay and Dave in their blog posts at www.gm4jh.com.

Sound bizarre? Get the book anyway for lots of follow-up ideas, then adjust them for what you think is appropriate for you—your situation, your personality, the people you want to make an impression on, etc. Remember, interviewers often get mixed up about who said what, who had what degree from where, who worked where. Too often we are afraid to do something unorthodox, but sometimes that's exactly what you need to do to stand out and be remembered! To show you really want the job and are excited about it!

In your follow-up you can say something like, "In our interview, you asked me how I would handle a rather difficult situation. I thought more about this question and wanted to add. . . ."

This allows you to add substance to your follow-up. You are continuing the conversation and showing your passion for the topic and role. Your continued conversation will likely make you more memorable. Isn't that powerful?

Whether you do something extreme or something dull, be better than 95% of your competition by following up, even if it feels a little uncomfortable.

SUMMING IT UP

As you understand the purpose of and prepare for interviews, you'll be more likely to make a good impression. Prepare for interviews by doing mock interviews as often as you think would be helpful. Practice answering common questions and creating mini-stories to help you stand out. Practice responses to questions that are hard for you, such as "Why did you leave your last job?" and "Where do you see yourself in five years?" And come prepared with questions that position you as the right candidate.

Make sure you follow up after each interview. Following up will give you a definite advantage. This is the time to shine, to stand out, and to be memorable.

NOTES

[1] Keith Ferrazzi & Tahl Raz. *Never Eat Alone: And Other Secrets to Success, One Relationship at a Time.* New York: Penguin Group, 2005/2014.

[2] Jay Conrad Levinson & David E. Perry. *Guerrilla Marketing for Job Hunters 3.0: How to Stand Out from the Crowd and Tap into the Hidden Job Market using Social Media and 999 Other Tactics Today.* Hoboken, NJ: Wiley, 2011.

YOU NEED TO WORK SMART ON THE RIGHT THINGS

Work smart, not hard, right? Kind of.

In your job search you need to work smart, on the right things. Don't waste your time doing tasks that get you no return or don't give you any value. Once you figure out that anything you're doing is not as effective as you thought it would be, stop doing it and replace it with something that is more effective. For example, if you send emails to contacts asking for time on their calendar, or letting them know how they can help you, and no one responds, look at rewording your emails. Maybe they need to be shorter or maybe you need to alter your tone. If you go to networking events but can't get a follow-up meeting scheduled, evaluate how you're communicating about yourself and/or how you're going about inviting contacts to a subsequent meeting.

So what about working hard? Your job search could prove to be one of the most challenging endeavors you'll ever undertake. For me, it was a massive mental game. I did things I would not have chosen to do if it weren't for the necessity of earning an income again.

The job search is a humbling experience. I went into it thinking it would be a logical, linear process. Do this thing, get that result. Repeat until you secure a job. What I found was that there are things you could do with fairly predictable results (like invite people to lunch, resulting in lunch appointments) but I was shocked by the emotions involved in my job search. Even if I knew what calls I needed to make and emails I needed to send, the self-doubt would set in, making those simple tasks feel impossible.

As I wrote on my blog,[1] being depressed clouded anything that should have been linear and logical. What should have been pretty easy work was confusing and discouraging, two things I wasn't used to.

Are you going to do hard work in your job search? Absolutely. For some of us, that means talking to people on the phone. For others, it will be dragging yourself against every bit of your stubborn will to a networking meeting, ready with a smile and an elevator pitch. Others will have a really hard time figuring out how to put a resume together or create other seemingly self-aggrandizing personal marketing assets.

I remember talking to a friend who scheduled multiple breakfast and lunch meetings each day during his job search. He didn't eat a full meal every time he sat down with someone—eating wasn't the purpose of these meetings for him. He found these one-on-ones over meals to be effective to nurture professional relationships, learn about industry needs and opportunities, and find out about job leads. He told me he kind of lamented landing a job because he had so much fun meeting people and talking with new friends.

The more you do the right things, the better you will be at them and the more enjoyable your job search will become.

Really, enjoyable. I know that sounds crazy, but your job search really can become a less stressful, even rewarding, part of your career and life.

I didn't find my job search enjoyable until I started working on JibberJobber. That was when I began looking forward to my daily tasks of networking and emailing people. I even looked at job opportunities differently.

Years later I was having lunch with Dick Bolles when he told me that when people understand they have options, they have hope. But when they don't see any options, they don't have hope. That resonated with me—once I saw more options, I had more hope, and with that hope came more joy in my job search.

Is the job search hard? Yes! Is it potentially enjoyable? Also yes!

When I first started my job search, I thought I needed to find a newspaper and look through the classified ads.

Seriously. That was in 2006! I knew there were online tools to help me, but I remembered, when I was growing up, hearing stories of looking for jobs in the newspaper "help wanted" section.

Don't worry, I didn't spend any time on that, even though I thought that was an important and relevant part of a successful job search. If you get job search advice from people who have been out of the job search world for a few years, you are likely going to hear advice that is outdated and ineffective. Much of the job search advice that's out there is not applicable to everyone at every level in every industry. The job search strategy or tactic that works for someone right out of school is likely not the same strategy or tactic a seasoned executive should implement. Looking for a job in a densely populated area like New York City or Los Angeles is different than looking for a job in a town of 10,000 people. What it takes to land a government job is usually vastly different than landing a job at a small, high-tech, funded startup.

Too often, advice I read or heard was too generic, and the phrase "one size fits no one" started to make sense. For example, the advice often given resumes. "It's a numbers game" is a common phrase used. The idea is that if you send out a lot of resumes, you are bound to get someone to reply. I have read multiple articles talking about people who have sent out thousands of resumes, or applied to thousands of jobs, and have not heard back from any of them. Sending out tons of resumes, or applying to lots of jobs, is almost always a frustrating and fruitless strategy, especially if you are sending out resumes just so you can feel good about the amount of resumes you are sending out.

Depending on your role, level, industry, target companies, etc., your job search tactics might look different than mine or those of other job seekers you have met. You need to determine if what you are doing is right for you in your situation.

When you do the right things, your self-confidence will grow. You won't spend energy wondering if you are on the right track, going through all the what-if scenarios, or changing your strategy or tactics so often that you don't give anything the time and effort needed to achieve results.

HIGH VALUE ACTIVITIES

Prior to the COVID-19 pandemic, I participated in a business development retreat that focused on how to grow your business. The retreat was conducted by Mark LeBlanc,[2] a consummate professional who was recently inducted into the Speaker Hall of Fame. I took pages of notes and was inspired by his wisdom, practical steps, and generosity.

One of the best practices Mark taught was to maintain our daily focus. He suggested grounding our day in our monthly goal and building each day upon three HVAs or High Value Activities. A High Value Activity is a business development step, usually one that can be done quickly.[3] Mark encouraged us to write down three HVAs each morning and then get to work. A High Value Activity could be as simple as making a call, sending an email, having a 30-minute Zoom conversation, attending a networking event, or having a coffee or meal with someone who works at one of your target companies.[4]

While you might consider getting organized, reading a career book, or calling a cheerleader to be high value activities, Mark would suggest that these are *valuable*, but not your *highest value* ways of investing your time, energy, and creativity. If you want to land a new job, what are the most important three action steps you can take today to get you closer to achieving that goal? These are your HVAs.

Each day, prioritize achieving your goal by taking the time necessary to work on your three HVAs. After you've completed your HVAs, then you can focus on other important tasks, obligations, and commitments. At the end of the day, your moment of truth comes as you report to your accountability partner how many HVAs you completed.

Mark reminded us that there will be days that get the best of us, and it's okay to have a bad day or one that is not as focused as we would like it to be. Possibly the pearl of wisdom that meant the most to me was his permission to reset our counter to zero every 24 hours and start all over again with three new HVAs. That means that today you don't have to make up for what you didn't do yesterday.

How liberating!

Mark's work is geared towards small business owners and primarily independent professionals. I asked him if I could borrow elements of his system and put it into a program for job seekers, and to my delight, he agreed. That effort turned into JobSearchProgram.com where I walk job seekers through six weeks of daily HVAs specifically designed for job seekers. In the Job Search Program system, when you report back, you can see a running tally of the number of days you have reported "yes" to completing your HVAs and the days you have reported "no," which gives you an idea of how well you are doing over time.

JobSearchProgram.com focuses on getting you up to speed on informational interviews and having the right conversations with the right people. That is, how do you get in front of hiring managers or influencers who can have an impact on getting you hired for the role you want? How can you have meaningful conversations that lead you to an offer or an introduction to someone important or influential at another organization? This is what I mean by having the right conversations with the right people.

So, what are activities that can be highly valuable to you, as a job seeker? Networking can be highly valuable. Networking with people in your industry or profession can be of higher value. Networking with hiring managers in your industry or profession can be of even higher value. Having an informational interview with one of these hiring managers, rather than merely connecting on LinkedIn, can be invaluable. See what we are doing? Not just identifying good actions to take, identifying the highest value actions you can take.

I love that Mark's system says to choose three HVAs each day. Three, that's it. They don't have to be time consuming and take up your whole day. Many of the HVAs I give you in the Job Search Program will take less than 10 minutes. The key isn't that you are putting in a lot of time, it's that you are doing things that get you closer to an interview, and *then* taking care of other routine and necessary activities.

In the Job Search Program, I tell you that if you need to do other job search tasks, do them! But at least make sure you do your three HVAs every day. There's power in consistently finishing tasks—if you are better at accomplishing the right actions and activities daily, you will build your self-confidence, gain momentum, and ultimately increase your odds of landing your next position or even dream position.

BUILDING CONFIDENCE

After my first book came out, I was offered multiple paid speaking opportunities. I'm no dummy. I had bills to pay, and honestly, it felt good for people to show interest in me after all of the rejection during my failed job search. I have a lot of good memories of amazing people I met as I traveled to speak, but the Twin Cities in Minneapolis will always have a special place in my heart. On one of my trips there, I spoke

14 times in three days. I didn't have a voice after that, but it was a great experience.

A few years later I was back in the Twin Cities. After a particularly fun presentation, a lady approached me and said, "Jason, I saw you speak three years ago. This presentation was way, way better than your presentation three years ago!" I was shocked because I thought three years ago I was pretty good. Even then, I continually received positive feedback and comments about how moving and inspirational my presentations were.

I spent the next few months thinking a lot about that woman's comment and came to one conclusion: Three years prior I had been scrappy, hustling, and frankly, worried about my fledgling business. Fast forward to my latest presentation and I was confident without being cocky. I was more organized and polished, and not as anxious in general. I was having a lot more fun in my career. I think she picked up on that, and it made my presentation much better for the audience.

Earlier in this book I talked about how HR can smell blood from a mile away. When you go into an interview, networking meeting, or any interaction regarding your job search, people will sense your level of confidence. As a job seeker, feeling hurt is par for the course. But there's a massive difference between someone who is a little hurt but still confident and someone who is wounded and has a lot of healing to do. Those you interact with will sense where you're at and may reflexively avoid you if it seems you are wounded and gravitate towards you if you are confident. People are more likely to give you introductions, which involves risking their own standing with their contacts, when they trust you aren't going to mess it up. If someone came to me and had zero confidence, I'd have a hard time introducing them to anyone in my network.

How do you gain confidence as a job seeker? Here are three things that have helped me:

1. Make your bed. I highly recommend watching Admiral William H. McRaven's 2014 commencement address.[5] It's one of the most inspirational videos I've ever seen. One message that stood out to me was the importance of making your bed every morning. He talks about how, despite all the things we do each day, we might not feel like we have accomplished anything—job seekers can relate! But he asserts that if you start your day by making your bed, you will have at least accomplished one thing.

There's power in accomplishment. Figure out what you need to do to feel accomplished, instead of continuously feeling, as most job seekers do, like you're spinning your wheels. Whether it's making your bed, doing 10 pushups, or eating a healthy meal, to build your confidence, notice and value your little accomplishments each day.

2. Expect rejection. Rejection is inevitable in any job search, but if you expect rejection and don't take it personally, you will be more confident.

One of the books that carried me through the rejection of my job search was *How to Become a Rainmaker* by Jeffrey J. Fox.[6] It's a fast read, and it's formatted in such a way that it's easy to pick up and just absorb a few short paragraphs at a time.

This book, written for people who want to have a successful career in sales, is also very applicable to job seekers—being a job seeker is very much like being a salesperson. The mindset of a salesperson, the tools, tactics, and methods sales professionals employ, can all be helpful to you in learning how to deal with rejection and in other aspects of your job search.

One unexpected form of rejection I felt was from friends and relatives critiquing my job search efforts. For instance, when I was doing things I was taught by career experts, like focusing on networking, and then told by people who were far removed from the job search that I should be doing other things, like sitting at home and applying to jobs online. They weren't rejecting me as a person, but I felt rejected as they second guessed the choices I made in my job search. That rejection caused me to second guess myself, which is something no job seeker needs more of.

131

In sales they say that no means no for now, not no forever. When you are told "no," telling yourself that "no means no *for now*," can be a powerful mental tactic that will help you avoid becoming discouraged. Maybe you ask someone for an introduction to someone in their organization and they put you off. That feels like a loud rejection, and you might be tempted to avoid asking that person for help in the future. But if you tell yourself, "no means no for now," after you've developed your relationship with that person, you may have positive results if you ask them for an introduction again.

The other mental tactic you can use when you feel rejection is to remind yourself that each no brings you closer to a yes. That feels really painful when it feels like maybe you need to endure a thousand nos before you get your yes. But the law of averages, even though declared as a false belief, is something that might carry you through rejections.

Accept rejection, figure out how to embrace it and not let it get you down, but also choose to learn from it. As you do these things, your confidence will grow.

3. Practice self-control. Let me share one of my favorite, most impactful phrases with you:

> Self-control builds self-confidence.

In my work, I get to talk to people who are in the depths of their job search, as well as people who have just landed their dream job. One of the most interesting phenomena I have seen, and experienced, is imposter syndrome. Whether you are in your job search or you are experiencing imposter syndrome at your new job, you have the same issue: self-confidence. So what does it look like to exercise self-control, and how will exercising self-control help your self-confidence?

Exercising self-control might mean forgoing donuts today. Or, taking it to another level, taking a month off of sugar. Maybe it means waking up a little earlier than usual or turning off your electronic devices at night and going to bed at a reasonable hour. Maybe you make sure you adhere to your exercise routine, do the hardest things in your job search first thing in the morning, or call a friend every day. Maybe you take a deep breath instead of responding in anger to a person who is annoying you.

Exercising self-control doesn't require starving yourself of fun or what fuels you. The idea is doing something worthwhile, even if it is difficult or out of the norm for you, maybe just to prove you can do it. As you exercise self-control by doing the difficult, uncomfortable things, your self-confidence will grow, even if it's just a tiny bit.

As humans, we tend to develop coping skills to deal with challenges and stress. Perhaps we bury ourselves in a book or binge-watch shows. Perhaps we eat or drink. We can even overdo it in the gym. I'm not here to knock how you cope, but I invite you to think about how you are coping during this immensely stressful situation and ask yourself if you need to make some changes that will help increase your self-confidence and help you perform more effectively in your job search.

Consistently, over time, that tiny bit of self-confidence will increase. How you interview at the beginning of your job search, when you are still processing the confusing emotions and working through your fear and anxiety, will likely be very different from how you interview a few months in, after you work on building your self-confidence.

OF RABBIT HOLES AND MISLEADING METRICS

Years ago, I wrote a blog post about a dog chasing a rabbit through a field.[7] The rabbit scurries into one rabbit hole while the dog, seeing dozens of holes, mistakenly starts digging at a different hole. The dog is solely focused on the hole he chose and doesn't notice the rabbit escaping from a different hole. Meanwhile, the dog exhausts himself digging in the wrong place.

Sometimes in our job search we can be like that dog. Our heart is in the right place and our efforts are admirable, but we are hyperfocused on doing the wrong thing in the wrong place. Or maybe doing the right thing in the wrong place or the wrong thing in the right place. Either way, our efforts aren't achieving results.

If your financial runway—the amount of financial leeway you have before you have to make serious changes, like selling a car or moving in with family or friends—is a year or two, you have time to spare and can explore various rabbit holes. But if your financial runway is only two months, you can't afford to waste much time going down the wrong rabbit hole.

In that case, make sure your job search is focused on networking, hopefully with a strong emphasis on informational interviews. Spend more time asking for introductions to and reaching out to the right people, rather than organizing your email, scrolling through social media, tweaking and retweaking your resume, and anything else you do that gives you permission to hide from what you know you should be doing.

Speaking of hiding, a friend of mine, John Davis, did a seminar for job seekers where he talked about chicken lists. John explained that the chicken list is the short list of people you are afraid to call or email. You might make progress getting through your task list throughout the day but keep putting off the two or three people you know you should reach out to.

John explained there is power in quickly working through your chicken list, contacting each person on the list. "What's the worst that could happen," he asked? It's not like they are going to reach through the phone and punch you. If contacting all 3 (or 100) people turns out to go nowhere, at least you'll no longer have a chicken list looming over you. Then you can move on to other tasks with peace of mind.

SUMMING IT UP

Too often, job seekers fill their days with busywork that doesn't get them closer to landing a job. But as you focus on High Value Activities, tasks that will get you closer to the right offer, you'll build confidence and make real progress in your job search.

Your job search will be hard, but can also be enjoyable!

NOTES

[1] Jason Alba. "Depression Clouds Everything." JibberJobber: Career Management 2.0. October 29, 2007. https://blog.jibberjobber.com/2007/10/29/depression-clouds-everything.

[2] Learn more about Mark LeBlanc by searching for his name on YouTube or viewing his resources at www.MarkLeBlanc.com.

[3] Mark LeBlanc, email to the author, December 7, 2023.

[4] See LeBlanc, Inc. "Mark LeBlanc - Club E Video." March 28, 2019. Educational video. https://www.youtube.com/watch?v=Sb8aAH1zkVU.

[5] The University of Texas at Austin. "Admiral McRaven addresses the University of Texas at Austin Class of 2014." May 17, 2014. Video. https://www.youtube.com/watch?v=yaQZFhrW0fU-.

[6] Jeffrey J. Fox. *How to Become a Rainmaker: The Rules for Getting and Keeping Customers and Clients.* London: Vermilion, 2013.

[7] Jason Alba. "2011 THEME: The Job Search Rabbit Hole." JibberJobber: Career Management 2.0. January 3, 2011. https://blog.jibberjobber.com/2011/01/03/the-job-search-rabbit-hole.

YOU NEED TO MANAGE YOUR CAREER

RETHINKING JOB SECURITY

When I was growing into an adult, I remember a lot of talk about job security. "Get a good education," "Get a job at a big company," "Be a good worker," "Don't rock the boat," and other advice was all shared with one purpose in mind: emphasizing the importance of having job security.

Back in the 1900s, job security was the notion that you could work at one organization for decades, retire there, and then receive a pension you could live on until you died. Having job security meant you could enjoy life outside of work, spending time with friends and family, pursuing hobbies, etc.

For about two decades now, I've been saying that there really is no such thing as job security anymore, and no one has argued with me. It's rare to find a person who believes they can work at a company for decades and then retire with a nice pension. Those days went away long ago.

My realization that we need to rethink job security led me to develop the concept that I call "career management."

CAREER MANAGEMENT

While job security is something that depends on your employer, personal career management is something that mostly depends on you. Yes, there are circumstances, like the cost of education and economic cycles, that will impact your career. But for the most part, career management is something you can invest in, work on, own, and see results from.

For years, my presentations about career management centered around networking, which we talked about in chapter one, and personal branding, which we talked about in chapter two. I didn't just choose those as the center of career management because they sound good or because a lot of other career pros talk about them. They are two core principles that are fundamentally necessary to managing your career.

I remember thinking, after about the hundredth time I gave my talk titled Career Management 2.0 (which is a Pluralsight course now), that I needed to update it. Was there another important career management element that complemented networking and personal branding? It literally took years, but eventually I discovered what element I was missing.

Income Security

That additional fundamental element of career management that I finally figured out is what I call "income security," which is a play on the phrase "job security." There's no such thing as job security anymore, but could we somehow create security in our income situation? The idea was to figure out moral, ethical, and legal ways to create perpetual income possibilities, the ever-alluring "make money while you sleep" idea. But beyond that, I came to realize that income security comes in the form of multiple income streams.

At the end of 2005, just weeks before I was laid off, I visited my parents with my young family. Late one night, while perusing the bookshelves, I came across the book *Multiple Streams of Income* by Robert G. Allen.[1] Over the next two days, I read and read. I just couldn't put the book down. I was intrigued by Allen's idea that having a high paying job was not the only way to create financial security or financial independence.

I was a general manager of a small software company at the time, and shortly after I returned home, I received a phone call in which I was told I was being laid off. I received a few weeks' severance pay and they let me keep my old work laptop, but all of those years I had invested in the company were gone, just like that. Because I had no other income streams, 100% of my income was gone.

I had given one entity control of 100% of my income. Sit on that for a minute. Over the next few months, I wondered why I had ever let anyone have control over 100% of my income. Why did I empower someone else to take all of my income away?

I had spent many years and lots of money, and put in all my blood, sweat, and tears, as they say, investing in my career. Only to let a boss, or in my situation, a committee (the board), take 100% of my income away. It felt ludicrous.

A few months later, I started JibberJobber with the goal of earning $100 a month. I was still hopeful I'd find a *real* job with a big company. JibberJobber was just a little side hustle, but that $100 a month would represent $100 my next employer could not take away from me. It would be income independent from my income at whatever job I landed.

Over the next few years, I grew JibberJobber into something a little more than $100 a month. I also wrote my first book, a book about LinkedIn, which ended up selling somewhere around 25,000 copies. My publisher had told me that if a business book sells 500 copies it is generally considered a success. I was pretty proud to smash that number. More importantly, I had created another income stream.

One day I got a call from someone who said her boss, the VP of a company that manages associations, "needed" me to speak at a conference in Florida. They simply wanted me to sit on a panel. That meant I'd be one of four people sharing two microphones. I wasn't really interested until they told me they'd cover all my expenses and pay me $5,000. I was definitely interested in earning $5,000 for spending 45 minutes talking about something I am passionate about!

Sitting on that panel was the beginning of my professional speaking career. As my book became more popular in the career space, I started receiving more invitations to speak at conferences and universities. I still laugh that I was paid to speak at universities that I most likely would never have been admitted to. I was also paid to speak at company meetings and consult with recruiting firms. Being sought after was quite enjoyable after my dreary job search.

Eventually, things slowed down with speaking engagements—there were new books about LinkedIn and fewer conferences being held. And that is when I was invited to create online courses for Pluralsight. Without going into detail, creating online courses that another company markets has been awesome, and it's easily one of my strongest income streams.

So that takes me to the beginning of 2018. I had created systems that freed up quite a bit of my time. I had so many cool things going on, so it might seem strange, but I started to feel bored. I had worked and hustled for a long time and was starting to feel some income stability, but my work wasn't as exciting as it had been. So I began to look for new opportunities. The next income stream I decided to pursue was, of all things, a job.

Getting this job was, in itself, quite a story, but not for this book. I was hired to work with one of the best bosses I've ever known, and I enjoyed every minute of my time with him. The project I was hired to work on would have changed the organization and provided a lot of value to our customers. It was exciting and unusual, and it seemed like my meandering career journey had perfectly prepared me for the opportunity.

Everything was great, for a few months. Then my boss announced he was leaving the company to pursue his longtime dream of starting his own company. What was going to be the best job of my life, and with significant earning potential, was slipping through my fingers. A few short months later, I found myself in my new boss's office getting laid off.

And here is the most significant part of this whole story. As my new boss told me the details of my layoff, my other income streams were top of mind. Yes, my boss was taking away some of my income. But I had worked for fourteen years to establish income stability, and it was paying off. More than half of my income would still be coming in when I lost this job, so my family would be okay financially.

Talk about feeling empowered! It was a fun point in my career! I had worked on the three elements of career management: My network, my personal brand, and my income streams. Getting laid off would have normally been a tragedy, but I was totally okay.

I was sad, of course, to not work with my team anymore. I was sad that what I had been working on was probably going to die. I was a little embarrassed to be one of the very few layoffs in that organization. But financially, I was fine.

I share this story to inspire you to build income security. I see people getting laid off again and again and going through this frustration too often, but with some time and effort, it's something that can be avoided.

OF VITAMINS AND PAINKILLERS

In my journey to understand both personal and entrepreneurial marketing, I've come across this concept of the vitamin and the painkiller.[2] I'll share what it is and then share two ways this applies to you in your job search.

When you have an acute pain, you typically want a painkiller to get rid of the problem. Have a headache? Take your favorite medicine to quickly get rid of the pain. We've become accustomed to quick solutions to rid ourselves of pain or inconvenience.

Vitamins are different. While some people take vitamin C when they have a cold, typically we don't think of vitamins as a treatment to resolve pain or inconvenience. If you take vitamins, you likely do so as a long-term preventative or system-building solution. You take them hoping you are building up your immune system to ward off illnesses in the future.

While painkillers are the first choice for resolving symptoms as soon as possible, vitamins are the first choice for building long-term health. Neither is necessarily right or wrong, nor better or worse. They are just different. Marketing vitamins is different from marketing painkillers. You need to understand what you are marketing in order to market it effectively. With that as a foundation, let me share how this applies to you in your job search.

First, you can incorporate this vitamin/painkiller idea into your own offering. Are you positioning yourself as someone who can develop strategies and systems to help the organization grow by multiples? In this case, you are the vitamin, strengthening them and preparing them for future issues. Or are you positioning yourself to go in and fix problems, resolve symptoms quickly, or take a pain away? In this case, you are the painkiller, the solution that can help them with an immediate and pressing need. Either way, figure out if you are more the vitamin or the painkiller and create the right messaging to accentuate your value.

The other way this concept applies to you is as a reminder that you need to take your career vitamins. I used to think getting a university degree was the last major, intentional thing I'd do for my job security . . . er, income security. I was wrong. I remember thinking after my job search ended, I wouldn't have to network, which felt very uncomfortable, or keep a current resume, until my next job search. I was wrong. I have since learned that networking, working on personal branding, and even creating multiple income streams are the vitamins. As we work on these tasks, over time and with consistency, we build a strong career foundation. We address root problems, such as having very few contacts in our industry, or being virtually unknown among our peers, before they become serious issues. And in the future, when we need to search for a job, we'll have a much easier time finding our next role, rather than having to start from scratch. Take your career management vitamins!

REVISITING GIVING AND TAKING . . . OR RECEIVING

In chapter one I talked about the importance of networking with an attitude of being a giver. People will appreciate your willingness to be open and share. They'll remember it and hopefully many people will reciprocate. When I switched from being a taker, or merely a consumer, to being a giver, I had more fun and saw results in my networking.

I want to talk a bit about being on the other side, which is being a receiver. Generally, being a taker is viewed negatively. Takers are viewed as weak moochers without any dignity. But most job seekers need to take what is offered to them; they aren't in a position to be proud. It's important to be service-minded and be on the lookout for how you can assist other job seekers. But it's also important to graciously accept assistance when it is offered to you.

I received a lesson on this when I went to a lunch appointment with someone in the tech space who I highly esteemed. Chris was a pretty cool guy who was well known and respected in our area. I was excited to get on his radar and chat with him about my situation.

We had a great conversation. Chris gave me some ideas, and, more importantly, he gave me hope and encouragement. Since I invited him, I planned to pay for his meal, but when it was time to pay, he insisted on paying. It was hard to accept, but this experience forced me to humble myself and realize that it's okay to be on the receiving end of assistance. I took Chris's advice, his encouragement, and I accepted him paying for lunch.

While receiving might feel uncomfortable for you, practice doing so with dignity and grace. If someone offers help, accept it. Something special happens to both the receiver and the giver when we accept help. And then, appropriately express your gratitude. Simply saying thank you acknowledges what you were given and shows your appreciation. Being ungrateful when someone helps you will discourage them from referring you to other people, whereas being grateful might lead to networking introductions and other help.

I HAVE TO DO WHAT?

Years ago, I worked for an entrepreneur who was a prolific writer. He had dozens of books to his name. Because of his books, and because he had done some interviews on Oprah and other outlets, he was known well enough, as he was apt to let people know, to be considered a celebrity. (He said there's a survey you can do and if your name reaches something like 3% of those surveyed, you are considered a celebrity.)

I worked for one of his companies that shared his main office space. He wasn't around the office much because he was usually on the road speaking and doing whatever celebrities do. But his executive assistant was. One day I walked through his office area and she had at least 40 manilla envelopes laid out on the floor. I asked her what they were, and she said they were his current book ideas.

I was amazed! This guy had already published a bunch of books and he was looking at a few dozen more! Maybe some of them were just titles and big ideas, maybe others were more fleshed out. Either way, I was impressed that he still had dozens of ideas he was working on.

Shortly after this experience, I saw him and asked about his future books. He told me that many people have good ideas ... book ideas, business ideas, whatever. But most people will never move from the idea stage to the execution stage. He said people who add value to society are those who take risks and actually take steps to implement their ideas. That's always stuck with me. As you manage your career, you'll have many ideas. But the real question is, will you implement your ideas?

I invite you to do just that—implement your ideas to make the world a better place. And as you do, you'll create multiple income streams and move towards income security.

SUMMING IT UP

As you make changes by applying the ideas in this chapter, you will see positive results. The changes I made were hard-earned and forced on me. But they were important. No longer am I bound by the whims of a bad manager or a fickle committee. My career management is in my hands way more than job security ever was. How empowering!

NOTES

[1] Robert G. Allen. *Multiple Streams of Income: How to Generate a Lifetime of Unlimited Wealth!* Hoboken, NJ: Wiley, 2005.

[2] George Deeb. "Is Your Product a 'Vitamin' or 'Painkiller?'" *Entrepreneur*, January 15, 2014. https://www.entrepreneur.com/starting-a-business/is-your-product-a-vitamin-or-painkiller/230736.

FINAL THOUGHTS

Inevitably, some people will put this book down and go back to the online job boards, spending hours browsing and trying to apply for jobs online. I hope that's not you! Hopefully the messages of this book have inspired you, and you're already applying what you've learned.

We need to change how we think about careers. Change what we think about education. Change what we think about the job search process, networking, and how we talk about ourselves.

Everything in this book, at least for people like the former me, requires a mindset change. I used to think that because I received a university education, and paid a pretty penny for it, I was, well, educated. On paper it works that way, but in reality, we need to keep learning.

I thought I'd do the hard work to find and land a job, and then work at the new job for a long time. I'd make enough money to build some kind of comfortable retirement and enjoy the journey along the way. (That's really hard to do when you get laid off every two to five years, which is what I've heard we should expect in our career.)

I despised the idea of networking for my career and talking about myself in what felt like a bragging sort of way. It felt superficial and self-aggrandizing. It wasn't who I was. Sure, I like people, but I like *my* people in my community. Going outside of my circles to grow my network felt uncomfortable.

I was firmly grounded in my mindsets. They were a part of my comfort zone. They were a part of my plan. And then everything changed. I had to learn that in one way or another, I'll be repeating the principles discussed in this book over and over throughout the years. And I learned I need to enjoy the journey.

I hope that as you've read this book, you have discovered which of your mindsets would benefit from changing. I hope it is firmly ingrained in your mind that you need to network with humans (principle 1), people need to understand who you are (principle 2), you need to be accountable (principle 3), you need to think macro so you can act micro (principle 4), you need to take care of yourself (principle 5), you need to master the interview process (principle 6), you need to work smart on the right things (principle 7), and you need to manage your career (principle 8).

I hope these eight principles will inspire you and give you the mindset and tools you need to have a peaceful, effective job search.

I believe in you. I believe you have value to contribute to this world. I believe you deserve goodness. Your job search won't last forever. You'll find the right next step for you. Perhaps the right next step will be a temporary job while you continue to look for the job you really want, perhaps it will be an entrepreneurial pursuit, or perhaps it will be landing your dream job. Whatever it is, you've got this!

If I can help in any way, please reach out at www.jibberjobber.com/contact.

ABOUT THE AUTHOR

Jason Alba is an entrepreneur, speaker, and author of several books. He earned a Computer Information Systems undergraduate degree and an MBA from Idaho State University. His career started in technology, as a programmer. Since 2006 he has been passionate about helping people in their careers, both job seekers and those who want to have more peace and success in their work. He creates online courses to help people learn and practice soft skills.

Follow him at JibberJobber.com and on LinkedIn at https://www.linkedin.com/in/JasonAlba.

www.ingramcontent.com/pod-product-compliance
Lightning Source LLC
Chambersburg PA
CBHW021403090426

42742CB00009B/984